Ziauddin Sardar is a writer, broadcaster and critical commentator on Islam, culture and science. Born in Pakistan and raised and educated in Britain, he is regarded as one of the world's leading public intellectuals. He is the editor of *Futures*, the monthly journal of policy, planning and futures studies, as well as co-editor of *Third Text*, the critical journal of the visual arts and culture. He is the author of over forty books on Islam, science policy, futures studies, postcolonial and cultural studies, travel and autobiography. His books include the classic studies *The Future of Muslim Civilization* and *Islamic Futures: The Shape of Ideas to Come*, as well as explorations of contemporary US politics, *Why Do People Hate America?* and *American Dream, Global Nightmare*. His recent autobiography, *Desperately Seeking Paradise*, offers an intellectual journey into what modernity means for Muslims. A columnist on the *New Statesman*, he is also widely known for his radio and television appearances.

D0061867

Also available

What Do Jews Believe? Edward Kessler

What Do **MUSLIMS** Believe?

The Roots and Realities

of Modern Islam

Ziauddin Sardar

Walker & Company
New York

Boca Raton Public Library, Boca Raton, FL

Copyright © 2007 by Ziauddin Sadar

All rights reserved. No part of this book may be used or reproduced in
any manner whatsoever without written permission from the publisher
except in the case of brief quotations embodied in critical articles or reviews.
For information address Walker & Company, 104 Fifth Avenue,
New York, New York 10011.

Published by Walker Publishing Company, Inc., New York
Distributed to the trade by Holtzbrinck Publishers

All papers used by Walker & Company are natural, recyclable products
made from wood grown in well-managed forests. The manufacturing
processes conform to the environmental regulations of the country of origin.

LIBRARY OF CONGRESS CATALOGING-IN-PUBLICATION DATA
HAS BEEN APPLIED FOR

ISBN-10: 0-8027-1642-3
ISBN-13: 978-0-8027-1642-2

Visit Walker & Company's Web site at www.walkerbooks.com

First published in the United Kingdom by Granta Books in 2006
First U.S. Edition 2007

1 3 5 7 9 10 8 6 4 2

Typeset by M Rules
Printed in the United States of America by Quebecor World Fairfield

For my late father,
Salahuddin Khan Sardar:
he understood

Contents

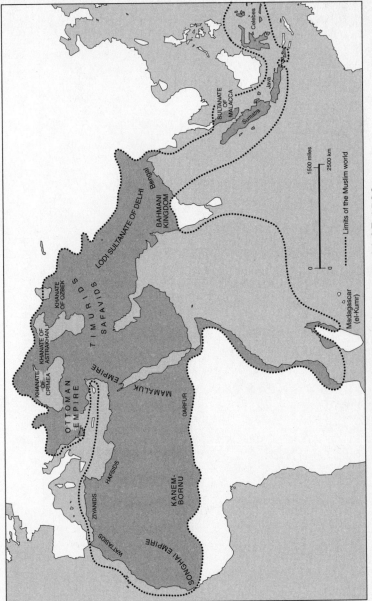

A Map of the Muslim World AD 1500

OTTOMAN EMPIRE

KHANATE OF CRIMEA

KHANATE OF ASTRAKHAN

KHANATE OF OZBEK

TIMURIDS
SAFAVIDS

LODI SULTANATE OF DELHI

Bengal

BAHMANI KINGDOM

SULTANATE OF MALACCA

Sumatra

Java

Celebes

MAMLUK EMPIRE

DARFUR

KANEM-BORNU

SONGHAI EMPIRE

WATTASIDS

ZIYANIDS

HAFSIDS

Madagascar (el-Kumr)

0   1500 miles
0   2500 km

••••••• Limits of the Muslim world

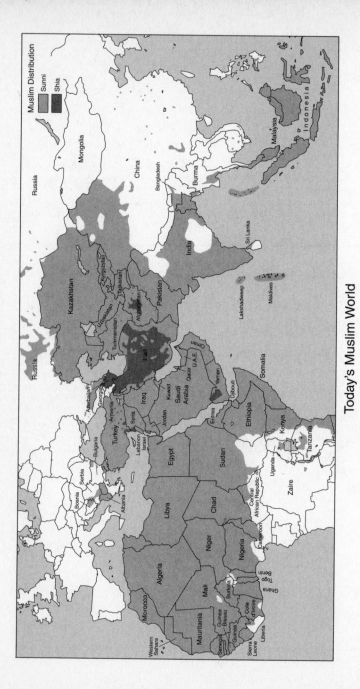

Today's Muslim World

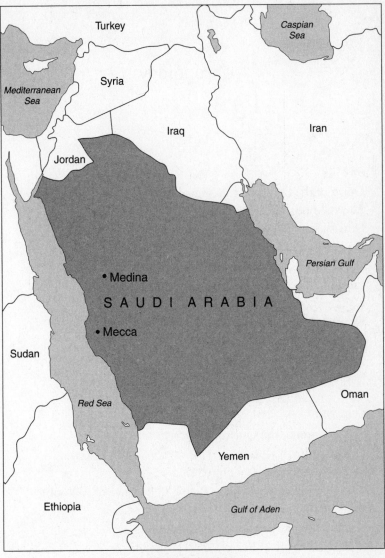

Turkey

Caspian
Sea

*Mediterranean
Sea*

Syria

Iraq

Iran

Jordan

Medina

SAUDI ARABIA

Persian Gulf

Mecca

Sudan

Red Sea

Oman

Yemen

Ethiopia

Gulf of Aden

Saudi Arabia

Chronology

632–49

Death of the Prophet Muhammad (632)
Abu Bakr becomes First Caliph (632)
Umar becomes Second Caliph (634)
Expansion to Syria, Iraq and Persia
Capture of Jerusalem (638)
Introduction of the *Hijra* calendar
Conquest of Egypt
Othman becomes Third Caliph (644)
Expansion into the Maghrib
Creation of the Arab Navy
Capture of Cyprus

650–700

Compilation of the Qur'an (650–52)
Defeat of the Byzantines
Ali becomes Fourth Caliph (656)
Proclamation of Muawiya as Caliph in defiance of Ali (660)
Assassination of Caliph Ali (661)
Umayyad dynasty established in Damascus
Muawiya I becomes Caliph (661)
Indian numerals appear in Syria

Introduction of Arabic coinage
Yazid becomes Caliph (679)
The battle of Karbala and massacre of Hussain and his party (689)

701–50
Invasion of Spain (711)
Expansion of Muslims into the Indus valley
Crossing of Muslims into France (718)
Battle of Tours (732)
Umayyad dynasty ends (749)

751–800
Introduction of the paper industry to the Arab world
The publishing industry established as a sophisticated enterprise
The great compilers of hadith publish their works: al-Bukhari,
Muslim, Abu Dawood, al-Tirmidhi, ibn Maja and al-Nasai
Abbasid dynasty founded
Al-Saffar becomes Caliph
Spanish Umayyads established in Córdoba (756)
Beginning of the Mutazilite philosophy (757)
Foundation of Baghdad (762)
Ibn Ishaq publishes the famous biography of the Prophet
Muhammad
Death of Imam Hanifa
Charlemagne's invasion of Spain; death of Roland (778)
Great Mosque of Córdoba founded; Harun al-Rashid becomes
Caliph (786)
Idrisids are established in Morocco (788)
Islamic jurisprudence (*fiqh*) codified with four 'Schools of
Thought' established

801–50

Ibn Hisham publishes his biography of the Prophet Muhammad
Philosopher al-Kindi established as the first Muslim philosopher
The first public hospital established in Baghdad (809)
Jabir ibn Hayan establishes chemistry as an experimental science
Imam Shafi'i dies (820)
Sicily conquered (827)
Al-Khwarizmi publishes *Algebra*
Bait al-Hikmah (House of Wisdom), public library, is founded
in Baghdad (832)
The translations of the works of Greece, Babylonia, Syria, Persia,
India and Egypt reach their peak
The Mutazilite (Rational) School of Philosophy founded
Thousand and One Nights makes an early appearance

851–900

Al-Jahiz, the 'goggle-eyed', publishes *The Book of Animals*
Philosopher al-Farabi publishes *The Perfect State*
Hunyan ibn Ishaq, the renowned translator, publishes
translation of Greek philosophy and other works
Mosque of ibn Tulun built in Cairo (878)
The *Ulama* established as a major force against the state
Philosopher al-Razi declares that functions of the human body
are based on complex chemical interactions
Musa Brothers publish their book of mechanical devices
Al-Battani publishes *On the Science of Stars*
Al-Fargani publishes his *Elements of Astronomy*

901–50

Death of Thabit ibn Qurrah, mathematician, philosopher
Historian al-Tabari, poet al-Mutanabbi born (915)
Death of Al-Hallaj (922)

Al-Razi publishes first book on smallpox and measles
Poet Firdawsi born (934)
Mathematician Abu al-Wafa born (940)

951–1000
Al-Haytham publishes *Optics*, containing the basic formulae of
reflection and refraction
Fatimid dynasty established in Egypt (966)
Al-Azhar mosque built in Cairo (970)
Al-Baruni publishes *India* and *The Determination of the
Coordinates of the Cities*
Poet al-Maarri born (973)
Ghaznavid dynasty established in Afghanistan and northern
India (977)
Philosopher and physician ibn Sina publishes *Canons of
Medicine*, the standard text for the next eight hundred years; and
many philosophic works
The publication of *Fihirst al-Nadim*, the catalogue of books
contained in the bookshop of al-Nadim (987)
Al-Azhar University, the first in the world, established in
Cairo (988)
The Ghurids succeed the Ghaznavids in Afghanistan and
northern India
Humanist al-Masudi lays the foundation of human geography

1001–1100
Statesman, educator Nizam al-Mulk born
Poet Umar Khayyam solves equations of three degrees
Theologian, thinker al-Ghazzali publishes *The Revival of
Religious Knowledge in Islam* and *The Incoherence of the
Philosophers*
'The Brethren of Purity' and other encyclopaedists publish

various encyclopaedias, including periodical part-works
Muslims travel as far as Vietnam, where they establish communities

1101–1200

Al-Idrisi of Sicily publishes the first detailed map of the world
Philosopher, psychologist ibn Bajja publishes *Ilm al-Nafs*, and
establishes psychology as a separate discipline
Philosopher, novelist ibn Tufail publishes *The Life of Hayy*
Ibn Rushd publishes *The Incoherence of the Incoherence* and other
philosophical works
Salahuddin captures Jerusalem (1187) and unites the Muslim
world, with Egypt as its centre
Al-Hariri publishes his linguistic masterpiece, *The Assemblies*
Yaqut al-Hamawi publishes his *Geographical Dictionary*
Poet Nizami born

1201–1300

Fakhr al-Din al-Razi publishes his great *Encyclopaedia of Science*
Mystic poet Jalal-al-Din Rumi publishes *The Mathnavi*
Biographer Abu Khallikan establishes philosophy of history as a
distinct discipline
Farid al-Din Attar publishes *The Conference of the Birds*
The Nasrids established in Granada (1230)
Mongols sack Baghdad (1258); the city's thirty-six public
libraries are burned down
Abbasid Caliphate ends (1258)
The Ottoman Empire founded (1281)
The Rise of the Mamluks in Egypt
Ibn Nafis accurately describes the circulation of the blood
Nasir al-Din al-Tusi completes his work *Memoir on the Science of
Astronomy* (1261) at the Maragha observatory, setting forward a
comprehensive structure of the universe; and develops the 'Tusi

couple' enabling mathematical calculations to establish a
heliocentric worldview
Islamic science and learning translated into European languages

1301–1400
Ibn Khaldun establishes sociology and publishes *An Introduction
to History*
Ibn Battuta publishes his *Travels*
Ibn Taymiyyah publishes his political ideas
Islam established in Indonesia and Malayan Archipelago
Mali, Goa and Timbuktu become important Muslim centres
Poet Hafiz, master of the ghazal, publishes his poetry

1401–1500
Death of Jami, the last of the great Sufi poets
Islamic science and learning begins to be incorporated in Europe

1501–1600
Mughal dynasty established in India (1526)
Eclipse of Timbuktu as the 'Great City of Learning' (1591)
Ottoman architect Sinan builds the Suleiman Mosque in
Istanbul

1601–1700
Taj Mahal completed in Agra, India (1654)
Islamic humanism adopted in Europe

1701–1800
British colonization of India
Shah Waliullah establishes resistance against the British in
India
Usman Dan Fodio establishes the Sokoto Caliphate in northern

Nigeria
Muhammad bin Abdul Wahhab establishes the Wahhabi
movement in Arabia, Syria and Iraq
Sayyid Muhammad bin Ali al-Sanusi establishes the Sanusi
movement in North Africa

1801–1900

'Indian Mutiny' (1857)
Jamal al-Din al-Afghani, Muhammad Abduh and Rashid Rida
establish the pan-Islamic movement
Sir Syed Ahmed Khan establishes the Muslim University of
Aligarh, India (1875)

1901–2005

Kemal Atatürk ends Caliphate (1914)
Rise of nationalism in the Muslim world
Poet, philosopher Muhammad Iqbal publishes *Complaint and
Answer*
Pakistan created as the first 'Islamic state' (1947)
Organization of the Islamic Conference (OIC) established (1969)
Emergence of OPEC (1972)
'Islamic revolution' in Iran (1979)
Satanic Verses and the Rushdie affair (1989)
End of Cold War, fall of Berlin Wall and emergence of new
Islamic states in Central Asia: Kazakhstan, Kyrgyzstan,
Tajikistan, Uzbekistan and Turkmenistan (1990)
Gulf War (1991)
Terrorist attacks in USA (11 September 2001)
Afghanistan War and fall of Taliban (November 2001)
Iraq War (2002–
Terrorist attacks in London (2005)

1

What Makes a Muslim?

'What does it mean to be a Muslim?' This plain and obvious question has both a simple and a complex answer. Let me begin with the simple explanation.

A Muslim is someone who makes the declaration: 'There is no god but God; and Muhammad is the Prophet of Allah.' This affirmation, known as the *Shahadah* – literally, 'witness' or 'testimony' – is all there is to being a Muslim. Anyone can become a Muslim, or claim to be a Muslim, simply by uttering these words. But beyond the declaration is the struggle to live by the spirit and meaning of these words.

The first part of the Shahadah, 'There is no god but God', declares the oneness of God. A Muslim is someone who believes in one omnipotent and omnipresent, and all-merciful God. As a basic principle, Muslims do not perceive God in human terms. Indeed, they argue that it is impossible for the human mind to comprehend an Infinite God who is responsible for black holes and snowflakes, the unconditional love of a mother and the havoc of a natural disaster. Certainly, God has no gender. But conventionally, Muslims refer to God as He (always a capital 'H'!). He is both transcendent and immanent. He has created the universe; and maintains and sustains it. The only way a human mind can understand Him is through His attributes. He is described as the Loving, the Generous, the Benevolent. He is the First (He was there before the 'big bang') and the Last (He will be there after the end of the universe). He asks us to love Him and to struggle to understand His will.

The second part of the Shahadah takes us from God to man: 'Muhammad is the Messenger of God.' How are we to have a reasonable understanding of an infinite, all-powerful creator we call God? For Muslims, the only possible way is for Him to communicate that knowledge by whatever means He deems fit. And throughout history, God has provided this guidance to humanity through various individuals whom He chose as His messengers. Prophets have been sent to every nation and community, beginning with Adam. Each prophet communicated the same message: 'There is no god but God'. The Prophet Muhammad communicated this message in its final form, and is thus considered to be 'the Seal of the Prophets'. A Muslim is someone who believes that Muhammad provides us with the ideal example of human behaviour and relationships.

To accept Muhammad as the Prophet of God is to accept that the revelation he received is from God. This revelation is the Qur'an. A Muslim is someone who believes that the Qur'an is the Word of God, complete and verbatim. Everyone who utters the Shahadah is duty bound to follow the guidance of the Qur'an. The principles and injunctions of the Qur'an provide the norms which shape Muslim behaviour and set the standards by which success and failure are judged.

The Shahadah is the essence of the Muslim faith – known as Islam. The word 'Islam' has the dual meaning of 'peace' and 'submission'. A Muslim is one who 'submits' willingly to the guidance of the One, All-knowing, Merciful and Beneficent God, and seeks peace through this submission.

But this submission is not an act of blind faith. Islam does not ask its followers to accept anything without question. Everything in Islam, including the very existence of God, is open to critical interrogation. Islam presents itself as a rationally satisfying faith. And the faithful acquire genuine faith only after they have pondered and reflected upon the 'signs of God' as manifested in the laws of nature, the material universe and personal experience of the Divine.

Just as submission cannot be blind, so peace cannot be attained without justice. In Islam, peace and justice go hand in hand. Submission is not a passive exercise. It requires all Muslims to struggle for justice – in society, in politics, at a global level and in their daily lives. So Islam and political and social activism are natural bedfellows.

There are two aspects of the Shahadah that have a direct bearing on how Muslims relate to each other as well as to non-Muslims.

First, the Shahadah incorporates a very strong ideal of human equality. We are all equal before God. No one, whatever their creed, colour, class, sex or persuasion, is superior or inferior to any other. This standard of equality, I would argue, is also extended to the notion of truth. Muhammad was a Messenger; but there had been countless messengers before him. Each community has some notion of truth which Islam recognizes and appreciates: truth is not the same for everyone. Moreover, Islam itself does not have a monopoly on truth – only the final formulation of truth which Muslims struggle to understand and live by with all their human limitations and frailties. Our understanding of truth is always partial, never complete. All communities, including communities without faith, are equal in their limited understanding of truth.

Second, the Shahadah promotes a positive view of life. God is the Wise, the Beautiful and the Subtle and He expects us to shape the world in His image. Islam argues that men and women are naturally inclined to do good – that is, promote equality and justice, to be fair and generous in everyday dealings, to be kind and gentle towards flora and fauna, and to protect and conserve their habitat and environment. Muslims believe that everyone is born pure and innocent, with innate beauty and the ability to rise to the highest level. Society, as a whole, has an infinite capability for advancement and for acquiring knowledge.

But, one could ask, are human beings not more inclined to be wicked? Are we not programmed to be unjust, to defy the ethical and the moral? Are we not, as Christians would argue, 'fallen' beings in need of 'salvation' before we can be expected to do good?

Islam's answer to this question is straightforward: no. We have free will. While human beings are naturally inclined to do good, they are free and quite capable of being wicked and unjust. But when they do so, they are acting against their natural disposition. It is the choices they make which define their actions as moral or immoral. If they had no choice – that is, if they were compelled, without freedom, to follow a single course – their actions would be neither moral nor immoral. Choice, resulting from free will, confirms moral responsibility.

We will be responsible, Islam teaches, for the choices we make in this world before God, after our death. Islam totally rejects the idea of 'original sin'. Whatever Adam did in Eden, he did himself. He repented his own personal misdeed and was forgiven by God. His actions do not cast a shadow on the rest of humanity. Unlike the Christian tradition, Muslims believe that we are not 'fallen', and so we are in no need of being 'saved'. We are not helpless; we have the freedom to choose good or evil. Our salvation – in this world and in the life after death – lies in doing good works, in promoting all that is noble, just and praiseworthy.

Why Is a Muslim a Muslim?

The Shahadah is perhaps the most frequently repeated sentence in any language. In the outlook to life which it engenders lies the answer to the second most frequent question: 'Why are you a Muslim?' In more general terms, we can rephrase the question as: 'Why is a Muslim a Muslim?' I, and I think most Muslims, are believers because we are inclined to see the world as a good and positive place. We also have a strong sense of equality and justice, which is further enhanced by our religion. And we wish equality and justice to prevail over God's earth.

Perhaps this is why Islam describes itself as a 'primordial faith', the natural inclination of men and women who are born in an originally good and pure state. Indeed, nature plays an important part in why a Muslim is a Muslim. Muslims do not only believe that we ought to live with nature, rather than try to dominate or subdue it, they also believe that the laws of nature do not violate the laws of religion. On the whole, Muslims do not try to justify their beliefs in terms of miracles.

Muhammad himself went out of his way to deny that he did or could perform any miracles. And the Qur'an invites not blind belief but an examination of the evidence it presents. In Islam, religious truth is a matter of argument and debate, a symposium in which everyone has the right to contribute, to convince and be convinced. I like to think that Muslims are Muslims because they like to argue.

This is why orthodox Islam has never had a Church or a Synod that could dictate what others should or should not believe. One arrives at the religious truth with one's own rational effort and endeavour. What happens next, how one lives by one's faith, is of course fraught with all sorts of problems.

This, then, is a simple delineation of what it means to be a Muslim. Now, for some complexity!

2

Who Are the Muslims?

Faith, like much else in this world, is subject to interpretation. Believers can *only* have an interpretative relationship with their sacred texts. My explanation of the Shahadah is, of course, my own – and some would legitimately argue idealized – interpretation. So it should not come as a surprise that there are many different, some even contradictory, readings of what it means to be a Muslim. Indeed, the sheer diversity of Muslims and verities of Islam can be quite bewildering.

We can appreciate the diversity of Muslims by looking at who they are and where they live. Geographically, Islam occupied what is known as 'the global middle belt'. From the shores of Senegal and Morocco to the Pacific Ocean and the islands of Indonesia. And, north to south, from the Mediterranean coast of Turkey to Somalia.

There are fifty-seven sovereign Muslim states. But there are also substantial Muslim minorities in non-Muslim states – India has almost as many Muslims as Pakistan and Bangladesh put together. And there are as many Muslims in China as in Egypt. And we must not forget the substantial Muslim presence in the European Union (around twenty million).

The Muslim population of the world is estimated to be 1.5 billion. That means every fourth person on this planet is a Muslim. They speak hundreds of different languages, and come from ethnic backgrounds as diverse as those of the Arabs and Turks, the Hausa and the Afghans, the Chinese and the Malays, the English and the Bosnians. Each ethnic community brings with it its own historical customs and cultural practices, which are often seen as part of their 'Islamic identity'. So, in Saudi Arabia Islam is defined in a very narrow and legalistic way and incorporates a number of tribal practices, such as the notion of unflinching loyalty to a clan. In Indonesia, where Muslims have been deeply influenced by Hinduism and Buddhism, Islam is described as 'tolerant and liberal'. Some Somali Muslims insist that the old custom of female circumcision is part of their faith even though the practice has no Islamic injunction and is totally rejected by the vast majority of Muslims. The mosques in China look more like pagodas than mosques.

Beyond the ethnic gloss lies a host of religious denominations. Muslims themselves recognize two main divisions within Islam: Sunni and Shia. The term Sunni derives from the *sunnah*, or the path, and the Sunnis see themselves as 'the people of the path'. They constitute the majority of Muslims and described themselves as 'the Orthodox'. The Sunnis believe that the first four caliphs who succeeded the Prophet Muhammad were legitimate successors and 'Rightly Guided'. Conventionally, the Sunnis belong to one of the four 'Schools of Thought', which offer different interpretations of Islamic law and jurisprudence.

The Shias are largely concentrated in Iran and Iraq. The term Shia means 'followers'. The Shias are followers of Ali, the cousin and son-in-law of the Prophet Muhammad. As we shall see later, the Shias' theology is somewhat different from the Sunni outlook. Here, it would suffice to say that, strictly speaking, the Sunnis reject the idea of a clergy. The Shias, on the other hand, have a highly organized clergy. There are equivalents of bishops and even a pope – the Grand Ayatollah. The Shia community has a number of divisions. The vast majority are 'Twelvers' who believe in Twelve Imams. A small minority are Ismailis who have their own, more esoteric interpretation of Shia thought.

Both Shias and Sunnis can be Sufis, or mystics. Mysticism has deep roots in Islamic history and the Sufis constitute a major division within Islam. Sufis believe that God is in all things and all things in Him. Moreover, all visible and invisible things emanate from Him, and are not distinct from Him. The Sufis are divided into numerous sects – or *tariqas* – ranging from the Whirling Dervishes of Turkey to the followers of the famous Andalusian mystic, ibn Arabi. Many new converts to Islam, particularly in Europe and the USA, are attracted to Sufism rather than orthodox Islam.

As if this diversity were not complex enough we have to add a number of other layers. Islam has been in turmoil for several centuries. Around the sixteenth century, the Muslim civilization, which was once a dominant, global civilization, began to decline. The pursuit of thought and learning was replaced by imitation – henceforth, the opinions of the classical scholars had to be imitated – and obscurantism. Then, many Muslim societies were colonized by European imperial powers. During the colonial period, a number of reform movements emerged, each aiming to galvanize the Muslim societies and revive Islam, each adding its own spin to the faith and its outlook.

There have been three such movements on the Indian subcontinent alone. The Tablighi Jamaat, which emerged in the 1920s, is an evangelical movement that believes Islam should be limited to rituals and have nothing to do with politics. The

Deoband movement, a breakaway group of Sunni Muslims, emerged from the Islamic university near Delhi from which the movement takes its name. It is overtly political. Its members fought against British rule and are now fighting 'Western imperialism' with equal zeal. The Deobandis are opposed by the Barelvis, who emerged about the same time from the Indian city of Bareilly. The Barelvis have turned the veneration of the Prophet into a high art – much to the displeasure of the Deobandis who shun all kinds of esoteric interpretation.

Perhaps the most noted of the reform movements is the Salafiyyah, which emerged in the Middle East at the beginning of the twentieth century. The Salafiyyah began as a modernist project aiming to accommodate Islam to the ideas of secular materialism. Despite its wide-ranging influence, its failure to introduce any substantial change in Muslim societies has now transformed it into an aggressive literalist movement based largely in the Middle East.

Followers of these and other reform movements have their own particular take on Islam. So do members of more recent and explicitly political 'Islamic movements' which acquired a global reach after the independence of many Muslim states in the 1950s. Such movements as the Muslim Brotherhood of Egypt and Sudan and Jamaat-e-Islami of Pakistan, as well as Islamic revolutionaries in Iran, equate religion with state. Their goal is to create an 'Islamic state' with Islamic Law as the law of the land.

What all this means is that there are as many interpretations of Islam as there are distinct Muslim communities. An individual Muslim may be a Sunni, a follower of one particular school of thought, a supporter of a political movement like the Muslim Brotherhood and may practise the customs of his country of origin, say Somalia. Or indeed he or she may be a Muslim who is, according to most orthodox Muslims, not a Muslim at all. The Qadyanis sect, which emerged in India during the Raj, has been declared 'non-Muslim' in Pakistan. Allegedly, the Qadyanis do not believe that the Prophet Muhammad was the last prophet. But, of course, the Qadyanis describe themselves as Muslims and perform all the necessary rituals.

This vast diversity and intractable complexity exists within a framework of overarching unity. Most Muslims share common beliefs and ritual practices that were established at the beginning of Islam.

So, let us begin at the beginning.

3

Where Do Muslims Come From?

Islam does not claim to be a new religion. It presents itself as a continuation of the religious tradition established by Abraham. Indeed, this religious tradition actually goes back to Adam. Adam, according to Islam, was not only the first man but also the first Prophet. So the followers of earlier prophets, Jews, Christians and others, were all, from the viewpoint of Islam, true believers in God.

Islam began in Mecca, Saudi Arabia, in the first decade of the seventh century. It was taught by Muhammad, son of Abdullah, of the tribe of Quraysh, which belonged to the clan of Hashim. When Muhammad was forty, he began to receive revelations from God through the archangel Gabriel. The revelations asked Muhammad to announce that he was the Prophet of God and to preach His message. Those who accepted the prophecy of Muhammad, and became his followers, were known as Muslims. The word 'Muslim' literally means 'one who surrenders to God'. The revelations were written down and became the Qur'an, the sacred text of the Muslims.

The life of the Prophet Muhammad is known as the *Seerah*. It plays a central role in shaping the behaviour, the thinking and the outlook of Muslims. To understand what makes Muslims tick, we need to know the basic elements of the life of Muhammad.

Who Was the Prophet Muhammad?

Unlike other religious leaders, such as Jesus and the Buddha, we know a great deal about the life of the Prophet Muhammad. He lived in the full light of history. His day-to-day activities, his dealings with others and his conversations were recorded during his lifetime, and extensive biographies were published soon after his death. So we have a rich reservoir of sources to enable us to appreciate and understand who he was and how he lived his life.

The Seerah literature is a unique institution of Islam. It is both history and biography, and a source for guidance and law. Conventionally, the Seerah is written in a standard, chronological form. It tends to concentrate more on the Prophet's battles and expeditions than his personality. I will follow the chronology, but offer my own interpretation of the Seerah by focusing on the personality of the Prophet.

Muhammad was born on 29 August 570 in the city of Mecca. At the time of his birth, Mecca was an independent city state dominated by the powerful tribe of Quraysh, who were largely pagans and polytheists. Located in a barren valley, Mecca was already a city of pilgrimage. It was famous for its temple which housed the Ka'bah, a cube-like building containing a black stone which is thought to be a meteorite. Muhammad's father, Abdullah, died before his birth, and his mother, Amina, died when he was only six. His grandfather, Abdul Muttalib, who was the chief of Quraysh, became his guardian, but he too died, just three years later. So Muhammad spent his youth with the family of his uncle, Abu Talib.

As an adolescent, Muhammad was very fond of solitude. He spent a considerable time in the desert and in the caves near Mecca, thinking and reflecting. He became concerned at the moral condition of people in Arabia: the idolatry, the lawlessness, the perpetual tribal and fratricidal warfare and, in particular, the practice of female infanticide, were an endless cause of agony. But he did not isolate himself totally from community affairs. As a young man, he was highly respected, living up to his name – Muhammad, 'the praised one'. He accompanied his uncle on business travels, visiting present-day Syria and Iraq. The Quraysh were so impressed by his honesty and integrity that they gave him the title of 'al-Amin', the honest.

When Muhammad was twenty-five, he was approached by a rich Quraysh widow, Khadijah, who asked if he would go to Syria on her behalf to conclude a business deal. Muhammad agreed and carried out the business transaction with his usual scrupulous honesty. Khadijah became besotted with the young man, so she asked another question. Would he marry her? She was fifteen years older than him. Muhammad agreed. The marriage gave Muhammad a much-needed friend and companion. They were a devoted couple, deeply in love. Khadijah was his refuge from the strife-ridden world outside, and she provided him with solace when he returned from his solitary reflections. They had four daughters and two sons – but the sons died as infants.

One day, Khadijah presented Muhammad with an unusual gift. She had bought a young slave, Zaid, son of Haritha. He had been captured in a tribal battle outside Mecca and brought to the city. Khadijah thought he would make a good son for her husband. So Zaid lived with Muhammad for a while. But when Haritha, Zaid's father, learned that his captured son was with Muhammad, he came to Mecca and offered a large sum for his return. Muhammad summoned Zaid. 'If he chooses to go with you,' he said, addressing Haritha, 'he is free do so.' Then he looked at Zaid and said, 'If he chooses to stay with me, then he is free to stay with me.' Zaid declared that he would stay with Muhammad, who treated him as though he were his only son. Then Muhammad took Zaid by the hand and led him to the Kaaba. There he publicly adopted him as his son and heir. Zaid came to be known as 'the son of Muhammad'.

By now Muhammad was approaching forty. He was becoming more and more disturbed by the conflicts and lawlessness, indulgence, cruelty and moral debasement that he saw all around him. He began to retire regularly to the cave in Mount Hira, a few miles from Mecca. He would usually go there alone; but sometimes Khadijah and Zaid also accompanied him. There he would spend all night motionless, thinking, reflecting, deep in meditation.

First Revelation

It was in the cave of Hira, in the year 610, that he received his first revelation. He was alone, tired, half-asleep, half in a state of meditation. A vivid light shone into his eyes, and he heard a voice:

'Muhammad.'
He broke out in a sweat. 'Who is it?'
'Read!' said the voice.
'I am not of those who read.'

Someone took hold of him, hugged him fervently and then
   released him.

'Read!'

'I am not of those who read'.

Again he was clutched and he felt as if his last breath was about
   to escape him.

'Read!'

He was hugged for the third time.

'Read!'

'What shall I read?'

'Read! In the name of your Lord Who created: He created man
   from a clinging form.

Read! Your Lord is the Most Bountiful One Who taught by
   [means of] the pen, Who taught man what he did not
   know.' (*Qur'an* 96:1–5)

Muhammad, trembling with fear, came down the mountain, ran all the way to Mecca, and went straight to Khadijah.

'Wrap me up, wrap me up,' he cried. Khadijah wrapped him
in a garment until his fear had subsided. He told her what had
happened, and expressed concern that he was becoming a
soothsayer or going mad. She listened attentively and then said,
'God forbid. He will surely not let such things happen. For
you always speak the truth. You are faithful in trust. You bear
the affliction of other people. You spend in good works what
you gain in trade. You are hospitable, and you help your fellow
men.' She paused for thought. 'Rejoice, O dear husband,' she
said. 'He, in whose hands stands Khadijah's life, bears witness to
the truth of this fact that you will be the prophet to this people.'
Khadijah went to see her cousin, Waraqa, a learned man who
had translated Jewish and Christian scriptures into Arabic. After
she had related an account of Muhammad's experience to

Waraqa, he cried out: 'Holy! Holy! Holy! This is the Holy Spirit who came to Moses. He will be the prophet of his people. Tell him this and ask him to be brave.'

Soon afterwards, the blind Waraqa and Muhammad's paths crossed on the streets of Mecca. 'I swear by Him in Whose hand is Waraqa's life,' said the old man, 'God has chosen you as His prophet. They will call you a liar. They will persecute you. They will banish you. They will fight against you. If I could live to those days, I would help you to triumph over your enemies!' Then he kissed Muhammad on his forehead.

After the first revelation, his biographers and commentators state, Muhammad suffered much mental anguish. But he continued his retreats to the cave of Hira where wrapped in meditation and melancholy, he received the second revelation.

'You, wrapped in your cloak, arise and give warning! Proclaim the greatness of your Lord; cleanse yourself; keep away from all filth; do not be overwhelmed and weaken; be steadfast in your Lord's cause.' (74:1–7)

Muhammad now accepted his role as a prophet. He started asking the Meccans to abandon idolatry, to give up the worship of pagan gods, and to accept one omnipotent God as creator. Khadijah was the first to accept his teaching.

The Prophet in Mecca

In the beginning, the Prophet was very cautious. He invited only those who were close to him to Islam. The second person to convert after Khadijah was the Prophet's cousin, Ali, son of Abu Talib. He was only ten at the time of his conversion.

Ali was followed by Zaid, the Prophet's adopted son. Then came Abu Bakr, a highly respected member of the Quraysh, renowned for his integrity. Soon afterwards, a group of fifteen leading members of the Quraysh embraced Islam. Included in the group was Othman bin Affan, a wealthy and respected merchant who, like Abu Bakr and Ali, was destined to play a major role in the coming years.

After three years of quiet but constant struggle, the Prophet had secured only thirty followers. Some of them were people of position and wealth, while others were simple, poor citizens. The small community of Muslims practised its faith in secret. But now the Prophet decided to communicate his message more openly. He began to address crowds of Meccans asking them to refrain from worshipping stones and statues and inviting them to the worship of one God. But his attempts bore no fruits. So he turned to strangers arriving in Mecca for trade or pilgrimage. Still, with no success.

The Quraysh were less than pleased with the activities of the Prophet. To begin with they doubted his sanity. They declared that he was mad or possessed by a malevolent spirit. But this had no effect on Muhammad. Then they started to issue warnings. If Muhammad did not stop attacking their gods, they said, they would be forced to take physical action. Finally, the Prophet's preaching evoked a furious outburst of persecution against him and his followers. They pursued him wherever he went and threw dirt and filth at him and his disciples. They scattered thorns in places where the Muslims offered their prayers. They stopped strangers before they entered Mecca and warned them to avoid Muhammad. They demanded that if Abu Talib could not stop his nephew from his activities, he should 'hand over his brother's son, who he has adopted, so that we can put him to death'. Abu Talib stood by his nephew.

When the sufferings of his disciples became unbearable, the Prophet advised some of them to seek refuge in the kingdom of the Negus. The king of Abyssinia was renowned for his tolerance and hospitality. So a small band of Muslims escaped to Abyssinia. But the Quraysh pursued them vigorously even there. On arriving in Abyssinia, the Quraysh envoy asked the Negus to hand over the refugees stating that they were guilty of abandoning their old religion and must be put to death. The Negus asked the exiles if the charge were true. The spokesman of the refugees was Jafaar, son of Abu Talib, and brother of Ali. His reply to King Negus is regarded as a memorable event in the history of Islam.

JAFAAR'S DEFENCE

'O king,' Jafaar began, 'we were plunged in the depth of ignorance and barbarism, we adored idols, we lived without morals, we ate dead bodies and we spoke abominations, we disregarded every feeling of humanity and the duties of hospitality and neighbourhood, we knew no law but that of the strong. Then, God raised among us a man of whose birth, truthfulness, honesty and purity we were aware. He called us to the Unity of God, and taught us not to associate anything with Him. He forbade us the worship of idols, enjoined us to speak the truth, to be faithful to our trusts, to be merciful and to regard the right of neighbours. He forbade us to speak evil of women, or to deprive orphans of their rights. He ordered us to flee from vice and to abstain from evil, to offer prayers, to render alms, to observe the fast.

'We have believed in him: we accept his teachings and his injunctions to worship God and not to associate

anything with Him. For this reason our people have risen
against us, have persecuted us in order to make us forego
the worship of God and to return to the worship of idols of
wood and stone and other abominations. They have
tortured us and injured us, until finding no safety among
them we have come to your country.'

Back in Mecca, the Quraysh modified their tactics. They
offered the Prophet wealth, anything he wanted as long as he
would desist from attacking their deities and spreading his message. The Prophet's reply was straightforward: 'If they placed the
sun on my right hand and the moon on my left hand, so that I
may renounce my task, I would not desist until God made
manifest His cause or I die in the attempt.' The Prophet's refusal
made the Quraysh even more angry.

But he too changed his tactic. In the face of increasing hostility in Mecca, he decided to take his message to the nearby
town of Taif. The inhabitants of Taif turned out to be even
more obstinate. They pelted him with stones and drove him out
of the city. Wounded and bleeding, he returned to Mecca to discover that the Quraysh were plotting to kill him.

More bad news greeted the Prophet. Abu Talib, his beloved
uncle, drew his last breath at the age of eighty. He died without
converting to Islam. Three days later, his loving wife and closest friend, Khadijah, also died. She was sixty-five. In these
darkest days of his life, stricken with double grief and threat-
ened by the Quraysh, the Prophet had his deepest and most
profound spiritual experience.

The Night Journey

Was it a physical journey or a mystical experience? Muslim commentators are divided on the question of Isra and Miraj – the 'Night Journey' and 'Ascension' of the Prophet. Some see it in rather literal terms, while other see it purely as a metaphysical voyage. But all agree that it was a central event in the Prophet's life. Like most spiritual experiences, I would argue, it is best understood in metaphorical terms.

Muhammad was in the area that later came to be known as the Sacred Mosque in Mecca, near the Ka'bah. 'Whilst I was sleeping Gabriel came to me. He led me out of the gate of the mosque, and there was a white beast, between a mule and an ass, with wings at his sides wherewith he moved his legs; and his every stride was as far as his eye could see. I got on his back and in a twinkling he carried me from the Sacred Mosque to the Mosque in Jerusalem. I alighted. A man appeared in front of me, offering a cup of milk and a cup of wine. I drank the milk and refused the wine.'

At Jerusalem the Prophet was met by a company of prophets – Abraham, Moses, Jesus and others. Then began the Ascension: led by the Archangel, the Prophet ascended beyond the confines of earthly space and bodily forms to seven Heavens. Everything the Prophet now saw he saw with his 'inner eye', his heart and soul. At the summit of his ascent was the 'Lote Tree of the Uttermost End', which is rooted to the Throne, and marks the end of knowledge of every knower, prophet or archangel. And the Prophet saw what the eye cannot see: 'His sight never wavered, nor was it too bold, but he saw some of the greatest signs of his Lord.' (53:17–18)

Soon after his 'Night Journey' and 'Ascension', the Prophet was approached by a party of twelve men from the city of

Yathrib. Located some three hundred kilometres north of Mecca, Yathrib saw itself as a rival city. The party, with ten members from the Jewish tribe of Khazraj, came to make a pledge. On the hill of Aqaba, in the northern part of Mecca, they took the following oath: 'We will not associate anything with God. We will not steal or commit adultery, nor kill our children, nor defame and denigrate others. We will obey the Prophet in everything that is reasonable; and we will be faithful to him in success and failure.' The party returned to Yathrib.

The following year, the group from Yathrib returned. This time there were seventy-three men and two women – some had converted to Islam, others had not. But all came with a single message: 'Speak, o Prophet! What do you want from us, for yourself and your Lord?' The Prophet was in great need of such assistance. His opponents had become so powerful and so enraged that he was in constant danger of his life. He thus decided to leave Mecca and move to Yathrib. The party from Yathrib returned to their city leaving the Prophet to arrange for his journey to their city.

The Migration

On 16 July 622, at the age of fifty-two, the Prophet began the *hijra* – his migration from Mecca to Yathrib. Accompanied by his closest companion, Abu Bakr, he travelled for three days, with the Quraysh in hot pursuit, and reached the city to a rapturous welcome. By now most of the city had converted to Islam. Men, women and children danced with joy in the streets. The city changed its name to *Medina-tun Nabi* – the City of the Prophet. The inhabitants of Medina received the noble designation of *Ansar* – the Helpers. And the Muslims from Mecca came to be known as *Muhajarun* – the Emigrants. A new bond was created between the Emigrants and the Helpers. All were bothers and sisters, duty-bound to help and support each other.

In Medina, the Prophet took two immediate steps. First, he built a small mosque together with houses for the emigrants from Mecca. Now, however, he was not just a Prophet but also a unanimously elected legislator of a prosperous city. (Medina was in fact a pluralistic city – apart from the emigrants and exiles, it had a well-established Jewish community as well as pagans and others.) Second, the Prophet issued a charter defining the rights and responsibilities of the citizens.

The charter began: 'In the name of God, the Beneficent, the Merciful. This charter is given by Muhammad, the Apostle of God, to all believers, whether of Quraysh or Medina, and all individuals of whatever origins who have made common cause with them, who shall all constitute one community.'

It went on to declare: 'The state of peace and war shall be common to all Muslims; no one amongst them shall have the right to conclude peace, or declare war against, the enemies of his co-religionists. The Jews who attach themselves to our community shall be protected from all insults and vexations; they shall have equal rights with our own people, to our assistance and good offices. The Jews of the various branches, and all others domiciled in Medina, shall form with Muslims one community: they shall practise their religion as freely as Muslims. The allies of Jews shall enjoy the same security and freedom. The guilty shall be pursued and punished. The Jews shall join the Muslims in defending Medina against all enemies. The interior of Medina will be a sacred place for all who willingly accept this charter.'

Medina was relatively peaceful for about two years. This period was used by the Prophet to establish the formal religious obligations of the Muslim community. The direction of prayer – known as the Qibla – was fixed towards Mecca. After an intensive discussion with the community, the Prophet decided that the human voice, rather than bells, should be used to call the faithful to prayer. The first person to make the *azan* – the call to prayer – was a young black slave, Bilal, who had suffered unspeakable tortures at the hands of the Quraysh. It was the habit of the Prophet to fast three days every month. But after a revelation, the fast of the month of Ramadan was instituted. The Prophet also established the obligation of *zakat* – giving a proportion of one's wealth in alms to the poor and the needy.

Towards the end of the second year of the hijra – which marks the beginning of the Islamic calendar – the Prophet received some disturbing news. A Meccan caravan of exceptional importance, with over a thousand camels laden with goods and arms, was returning from Syria. The leader of the caravan, Abu Safyan, feared that it would be attacked by the Muslims. So he asked the Meccans for an army to protect the caravan. The Quraysh took little time to marshal a large, well-equipped force. But their intention was not just to protect the caravan – they planned to march against Medina.

The Prophet realized that he had little choice but to face the Meccan army. He chose to fight the battle not in Medina but in the nearby well of Badr. This gave the Muslims a strategic advantage: access to water. On one side were 313 ill-equipped Muslims, with seventy camels and three horses. They faced a mighty Quraysh army of 950 men, seven hundred camels and a hundred horses. The battle was swift – lasting less than half a day – and the Muslim victory decisive. Around seventy Meccans, including a string of leaders, were killed; seventy-five were taken prisoner. The Prophet issued an order that the prisoners should be treated with the utmost respect and dignity.

The following year – 625 – the Meccans returned to avenge their defeat at Badr. This time they were three thousand strong. The Prophet could only muster an army of seven hundred, with only one horse to share between them. This time the battle was fought at Mount Uhad, around five kilometres from Medina. Once again the Prophet secured a strategic advantage. He placed fifty archers on the top of the mountain. The Muslims repelled the Meccan infantry. Thinking that they had won, the archers abandoned their position. The Meccans regrouped and attacked from behind. In the resulting battle, the Prophet himself was wounded. Some seventy Muslims were killed. But the battle did not have a decisive outcome, and by evening the Meccans withdrew.

The Quraysh, however, were not ready to give up. They returned two years later, this time with an army of ten thousand – the largest force ever seen in Arabia. On the advice of one of his companions, the Prophet dug a wide trench all around Medina. The Meccans made repeated attempts to cross the trench but failed. Unused to long sieges, and short of food and water, the Meccan army started to lose heart and drift away. Then, around two months into the siege, there was a huge storm. The Meccans decided to cut their losses, and returned home. The so-called 'battle of the ditch' was in fact not a battle at all.

Hudaybiya Agreement

When the siege was over, the Prophet decided to make a pilgrimage to Mecca. He led a group of sixteen hundred men. They were mostly unarmed and wore the pilgrim dress of two seamless garments. The Prophet also sent an envoy to Mecca to inform its citizens of his peaceful intention and to seek permission to enter the city for *hajj*, the pilgrimage to Mecca.

Initially, the Meccans wanted to fight and drive the Muslims back. But eventually they chose to negotiate and sign a pact.

The agreement was drawn up at Hudaybiya, a settlement fifteen kilometres west of Mecca. According to Muslim sources, the following dialogue took place between the Prophet and Suhayl ibn Amr, who was negotiating on behalf of the Meccans.

'Ali,' said the Prophet, 'write: In the name of Allah, the Merciful, the Compassionate.'

'I cannot accept that wording,' protested Suhayl.

The customary 'In your name, Allahumma' had to be used.

The Prophet agreed and continued, 'It has been agreed between the undersigned, Muhammad, the Messenger of God . . .'

Suhayl interrupted. 'If I acknowledge that you are the Prophet of Allah, then I would not be at war with you.'

This time the Muslims protested angrily, and swords were drawn, and Ali refused to cross out what he had written. The Prophet took the pen and himself crossed out the words 'Messenger of Allah'.

'Well then,' he said, 'write: between Muhammad ibn Abdullah and Suhayl ibn Amr. Hostilities will cease for a period of ten years. Anyone escaping from Mecca and taking refuge with Muhammad shall be given up to the Quraysh. Muhammad and his followers will turn back and not attempt to enter Mecca against the will of the Quraysh. Next year the Quraysh will cease all opposition to the visit of the Muslims to the Holy Places for three days, but carrying only the arms permitted to pilgrims: sheathed swords.'

When his companions heard these clauses, which placed Muslims at serious disadvantage, they were upset. 'Prophet,' they said, 'would you sign such a treaty?'

'Assuredly,' the Prophet replied.

Before the Prophet could put his signature on the treaty, a young man burst through the Meccan ranks. He was Abu Jandal, son of Suhayl ibn Amr. He had converted to Islam and had been tortured and imprisoned. He rushed towards the Muslims, dragging around his ankle the links of his broken chain.

When Suhayl saw his son, he lashed out at him. Then, seizing him by his garment, he dragged him towards the Prophet. 'O Muhammad,' he said, 'here is the first fugitive. I call on you to hand him over to me.'

The Muslims were forced to stand by as Abu Jandal was dragged away.

'Am I to be returned to the polytheists who persecute me for my religion? See what they have done to me,' cried Abu Jandal.

The Muslims returned to Medina. They had not performed the hajj. And by the very treaty they had signed, they could not help Abu Jandal and others like him. Many thought that this was a serious setback. But the Qur'an declared that the Hudaybiya agreement was a great victory. 'Truly we have opened up a path to clear triumph for you.' (48:1) It established the principle that sometimes compromise, however uncomfortable, is necessary to secure peace, that intransigence is not conducive to viable negotiations. And what may appear to be a setback, can be turned, through peaceful means, into a triumph.

Return to Mecca

The treaty only lasted two years. The Quraysh violated its terms and, when reminded by the Prophet of their obligations, declared it null and void. So, on 11 January 630, the Prophet led an army of ten thousand men to Mecca. The demoralized Meccans offered no resistance. Before entering the city in triumph, the Prophet forbade his soldiers from fighting. The people who had pursued him with unrelenting hatred, persecuted him relentlessly, tortured and murdered his followers, waged wars against him and sought to destroy him by every possible means, were now at his mercy.

When the Meccans gathered in front of him, the Prophet asked, 'What do you say now? And what do you think now?'

They replied, 'We say well, and we think well.'

The Prophet ordered a general amnesty saying, 'You will hear no reproaches today. May God forgive you: He is the Most Merciful of the merciful.' (12:91)

The Quraysh were treated with kindness and generosity that has no parallels in history. No house was robbed. No man or woman was molested. There was only truth and reconciliation.

The Quraysh wanted the Prophet to settle in Mecca. But he chose to return to Medina which now became the capital of an expanding Muslim polity. Life was hectic as tribe after tribe came to pay allegiance to the Prophet. They were always received with consideration and treated with hospitality. A written treaty guaranteeing the privileges of the tribes was always granted to the deputies. For example, the Prophet granted a charter to the Christians who lived within the boundaries of the Muslim rule. It read:

To the Christians of Najran and the neighbouring territories: the security of God and the pledge of His Prophet are extended for their lives, their religion and their property – to the present as well as the absent and others besides. There shall be no interference with [the practice of] their faith or their observances, nor any change in their rights or privileges. No bishop shall be removed from his church, nor any monk from his monastery, nor any priest from his priesthood. And they shall continue to enjoy everything great and small as before. No image or cross shall be destroyed. They shall not oppress or be oppressed. No tithes shall be levied from them, nor shall they be required to furnish provision for the troops.

The Prophet also sent envoys and missionaries to other communities. Every missionary received the same advice: 'Deal gently with the people, and be not harsh, cheer them, and condemn them not. You will meet many People of the Book [Jews and Christians] who will ask you: "What is the key to Heaven?" Reply to them: "The key to Heaven is to testify to the truth of God, and to do good works."'

Less than ten years after the hijra, the Prophet had united most of Arabia. He was past sixty and was beginning to feel his age. In March 632, he performed his last pilgrimage to Mecca; and from the top of Mount Arafat, addressed the Muslims for the last time.

FROM THE PROPHET'S 'FAREWELL ADDRESS'

O people, listen to my words, for I know not whether I will be with you for another year. Your lives and property are sacred and inviolable amongst one another. Remember that you will appear one day before your God Who shall demand from you an account of all your actions. Wrong not and you shall not be wronged. You have rights over your wives, and your wives have rights over you so treat them with kindness. Know that all Muslims are brothers, and you are one brotherhood. You are all equals, and enjoy equal rights and have similar obligations. Nothing that belongs to another is lawful unto his brother, unless freely given out of goodwill. Guard yourselves from committing injustice. Do not tyrannise your people; and do not usurp their rights. Let those who are present tell those who are absent. Perhaps those who are told afterwards may remember better than those who have heard it now.

On Monday 8 June 632, while praying in whispers, the Prophet died. His last words: 'O Allah, with the Compassionate on High.'

The life of the Prophet Muhammad, known as the Seerah, is central to the beliefs, thought and actions of Muslims. I have presented the main features of the Seerah, while concentrating on the personality of the Prophet. There are, however, some aspects of the Seerah which can be seen as 'problematic'.

Certain Western writers have accused Muhammad of being prone to violence. But this accusation, perpetuated throughout history to such an extent that it has now become a standard Western stereotype, is a myth. To some extent, the way the Seerah has been written by Muslims, with its overemphasis on the battles of the Prophet, has also enhanced this myth. In fact, during the sixty-three years of his life, the Prophet spent less than a couple of months fighting. The major battles of his life, the battles of Badr and Uhad, lasted less than a day. The other engagement with the Quraysh, the battle of the trenches, did not result in combat. The conquest of Mecca was largely a peaceful affair. Indeed, the clear evidence is that the Prophet abhorred violence and went out of his way to avoid it. However, when it became a question of basic survival, he was forced to come out fighting.

The other accusations concern the Prophet's wives. The

Prophet married eleven times. This is seen as a clear evidence of his 'lust'. But before we jump to conclusions, a few points need to be considered. The Prophet lived during an era when polygamy was the norm. This is why most of the Biblical prophets had multiple wives. But there was another incentive for polygamy: in Arabia marriage was the normal route to bringing two warring tribes together, to forge alliances, and to unite a land driven by strife and conflict. This is what most of the Prophet's marriages were designed to do: they were marriages of political alliance.

Muhammad's first wife, as we have seen, was the twice-widowed Khadijah, who was fifteen years older than him. As long as Khadijah was alive, the Prophet remained monogamous. Khadijah was also the only wife to bear him children. After her death, the Prophet married Sawdah, the widow of one of his companions. Then followed his marriage to Aisha, which is seen as the most contentious. Aisha, daughter of his closest friend Abu Bakr, was only six. But the marriage was not consummated, and the Prophet lived separately from her, until she came of age, many years later after the hijra. And Aisha, one of the most articulate and open-minded women of early Islamic history, was more than happy with the union. Virtually all the other wives of the Prophet were widows. There is, though, one exception: Zaynab, who divorced the Prophet's freed slave, Zaid, to marry him. This was not uncommon in those days; men and women divorced each other freely to marry others. She was forty, he was sixty; and there was a strong personal attraction between the two.

What the Seerah, including the marriages, suggest is that the Prophet was very human and very humane. Muslims sometimes forget that the Prophet was a human being, and try to deify him. But it is his humane virtues that should be the focus of attention.

The immediate successors to the Prophet also exhibited these humane qualities. The first four – Abu Bakr, Umar, Othman and Ali – have come to be known as 'the rightly guided caliphs'. Their biographies shaped the formative phase of Muslim history and have become a site of dispute – particularly amongst Shias and Sunnis. Muslims hold these personalities in high regard and the Seerah is often related in conjunction with the lives of the rightly guided caliphs. As such, these biographies constitute an important part of the Islamic worldview.

Who Were Muhammad's Main Disciples?

When the Prophet's death was announced in 632, a crowd gathered around his house. 'How can our Prophet be dead?' they exclaimed. 'No, he is not dead,' said Umar. 'He will be restored to us. Those who say he is dead are traitors to Islam.'

Umar bin Khattab was one of the closest companions of the Prophet. A respected, highly learned and literary figure, he belonged to the tribe of Adiyy, which occupied a position of distinction amongst the Quraysh. He converted to Islam during 615, shortly after a small group of Muslims left Mecca to seek refuge in Abyssinia. One day, the story goes, the fierce Umar heard his brother-in-law reciting the Qur'an. He burst into his sister's house in anger and demanded: 'What is this recitation in an undertone that I heard, and which you cut short when I arrived?'

Eventually, Umar secured the parchment on which he read: 'Ta Ha. It was not to distress you [Prophet] that we sent down the Qur'an to you, but as a reminder to those who hold God in awe, a revelation from the One Who created the earth and the high heaven, the Lord of Mercy, established on the throne.'

(20:1–5) Umar could not contain himself. 'How beautiful! What sublime language!' He asked to be taken to the Prophet; and he converted soon afterwards.

When the news of the Prophet's death was announced, Abu Bakr, who was amongst the first to convert and remained at his side throughout his life, was in his house in the As-Sunah quarter of Medina. He came galloping on his horse, alighted, and went straight into the Prophet's mosque without speaking. He kissed the Prophet and wept. Shortly afterwards he came out and went straight to Umar. 'Sit down, Umar,' he said. Umar refused to obey him. Abu Bakr then addressed the crowd. 'O believers,' he began, 'if you worshipped Muhammad know that Muhammad is dead. But whosoever worshipped God, know that God is alive, for He cannot die.' Then he recited the following verse of the Qur'an: 'Muhammad is only a messenger before whom many messengers have been and gone. If he died or was killed, would you revert to your old ways?' (3:144)

When Umar heard Abu Bakr he began to tremble. 'By Allah,' he later said, 'when I heard Abu Bakr recite these verses I felt my legs give way under me. I was about to fall down – and I understood that the Prophet was really dead.'

When Umar recovered from his grief he suggested that Abu Bakr be elected the Prophet's successor. There were other contenders. Abu Bakr himself nominated Umar. Then there was Othman bin Affan who was among the first group of fifteen Quraysh to convert to Islam. And, of course, the Prophet's beloved cousin and son-in-law, Ali. But Umar argued that Abu Bakr had been the closest to the Prophet during the days of persecution and hardship in Mecca. And was he not the only one who accompanied the Prophet during the hijra? Did he not lead the prayers when the Prophet was too ill?

There was considerable debate and discussion. But Umar's opinion carried the day. So Abu Bakr became the first successor to the Prophet, or First Caliph of Islam.

Abu Bakr

After his unanimous election, Abu Bakr gave the following speech. 'I have been chosen by you as your leader, although I am no better than any one of you. If I do good, give me your support. If I do any wrong, set me right . . . The weak among you are the powerful in my eyes, as long as I do not get them their dues. The powerful among you are the weak in my eyes, as long as I do not take away from them what is due to others . . . Obey me as long as I obey Allah and His messenger. If I disobey Allah and His messenger, you are free to disobey me.'

Abu Bakr was a simple and very pious man. His real name was Abdullah, but he was more widely known as 'Siddiq', the truthful, and 'Atiq', the generous. Ever ready to give all he had to the needy, he was frequently seen selling bundles of clothes in the market, even after he was elected Caliph. Umar tried to persuade him to give up his trade and insisted that the public treasury should provide him with a 'middling pension'. He agreed to a stipend of one garment for winter, one for summer, and some lamb meat each day for food. He would stop people in the streets and ask if they had any complaints against him. Renowned for treating his subordinates with the utmost respect and consideration, he would frequently be seen walking while they rode their mounts. As a ruler, he would not make any decisions without consulting his people. His greatest joy was playing with children and milking the goats of orphans and widows.

Abu Bakr served as Caliph for just two years and three months. He moved swiftly to reassert unity amongst the Muslim tribes, seeking to make the bonds of common religion predominate over tribal kinship. He quelled a rebellion among some tribes who refused to pay zakat, and he sent expeditions to Palestine, Syria and Iraq. When he died in 634, he left a stable state and a flourishing society as well as the nucleus of an emerging global civilization.

After consulting with senior Companions of the Prophet, Abu Bakr nominated Umar as his successor. But the nomination was subject to the approval of the majority. Abu Bakr's nomination, which he embodied in an ordinance dictated to Othman, was therefore put before the people in the Prophet's mosque. It was readily approved. So, after the death of Abu Bakr, Umar became the Second Caliph of Islam.

Umar

Umar ibn Khattab had a strong sense of justice. Hence his honorific title, al-Farooq – the just. A consummate orator, he possessed great administrative skills. During Umar's reign (634–44), the Muslim empire expanded to Syria, Palestine, Egypt and Persia. Umar developed a sophisticated structure for the administration of the rapidly expanding Muslim polity.

He established two consultative bodies. There was a General Assembly, convened by making a general announcement throughout the state, to which every citizen was entitled and where affairs of national interest were discussed. For the day-to-day running of the state, Umar set up an Advisory Council of Representatives. Cities, tribes and non-Muslim communities were asked to send representatives. He also insisted that governors of cities and regions should be chosen by the inhabitants of the area. Attached to the office of the governor was a special bureau where citizens could take their complaints and grievances against the governor. The independent bureau had the power to remove the governor.

Umar also established an elaborate system of collecting taxes and distributing welfare. He introduced tax on private property, agricultural productivity and a tax in lieu of military service paid largely by non-Muslims. In return, senior citizens received a pension, widows and the needy received social security, and every child received state benefit. These applied equally to Muslims and non-Muslims. A major census was undertaken to establish who was entitled to various benefits.

For Umar, the office of the Caliph was not an office of grandeur or self-promotion. He saw himself as a servant of the people. If the camels of the public treasury were taken ill, there was the Caliph applying the necessary treatment with his own hands. When Arabia was stricken by famine, Umar carried sacks of corn on his own back to distribute to the people.

Often, he would go out at night to see for himself how his people were fairing. On one such visit, he heard the cries of a woman from a tent. On inquiring, he was informed that the woman was alone and was in labour, but there was no one to attend to her. He hurried back to his house and took his wife to the tent to nurse her.

During the time of the famine, he found a woman with nothing to eat. Her children were crying. To console them, she had put a pot on the fire with nothing but water in it. When Umar saw this, he went back and returned with a bag of flour on his back. When an official offered to carry the load for him, he replied, 'In this life you might carry my burden for me, but who will carry my burden on the Day of Judgement?'

He forbade his commanders and governors from holding property outside the Arabian peninsula and exhorted them to treat their people with total equality. When he heard that Amr ibn As, the governor of Egypt, had built a pulpit for himself in the mosque, he sent a short, sharp letter. Remove the pulpit, he wrote, for it is not proper for one man to sit above all others.

When Umar arrived in Jerusalem, after the city fell to the Muslims in 638, he was on foot and wearing his usual ordinary clothes. This caused a great deal of astonishment among the local Greek Christian population, who were used to the pompous ceremonies of the Byzantine emperors. He assured the Patriarch that the sanctity of all Christian institutions will be preserved. The Patriarch then showed him around various places of pilgrimage in the city. The time for one of the daily prayers came while he was visiting the Church of the Resurrection. The Patriarch suggested that he could offer the prayers there. But Umar declined politely. He explained that his example might later be followed by Muslims and they might try to convert the place into a mosque.

Umar was fatally stabbed in 644 at the age of fifty-three. Before he died, he appointed an Electoral Council of six Companions of the Prophet to choose his successor. The council was ordered to consult the chiefs of all the clans as well as prominent members of the Muslim community. On his deathbed, Umar advised his successor to take particular care of the rights of the non-Muslim subjects. The council chose Othman bin Affan.

Othman

Othman was already seventy when he was elected Caliph. His first act was to write to the governors throughout the empire reminding them to be just. 'Even to your enemies,' he wrote, 'your conduct must be upright. Win them with your good conduct and fulfilment of promises.'

A highly successful businessman, he declined to take even a nominal salary from the public treasury. During his reign of twelve years, the Muslim empire expanded rapidly reaching Cyprus, North Africa and as far as Afghanistan in Asia. Muslims also developed a navy, which was built in the shipyards of Egypt and Syria. The expanding Muslim empire became wealthy and the wealth brought considerable discord with it. So Othman's Caliphate also saw considerable unrest, uprisings and outright rebellion. During all this tumultuous time, Othman never lost his poise or his temper, and always behaved with equanimity. By far his greatest achievement was the production of an authorized written edition of the Qur'an, completed by 652.

Othman was murdered while reading the Qur'an in 656. He was succeeded by Ali ibn Abu Talib, the Prophet's cousin.

Ali

Ali had married, Fatimah, one of the Prophet's daughters, and the couple lived a very austere life. An exceptionally brave and courageous man, Ali was renowned for his learning. His sermons, letters and sayings have been collected in *Nahj al-Balagha*, which is an important source of guidance for Shia Muslims.

Ali's reign lasted five years. He moved the capital of the Muslim empire to Kufa in Iraq. It was a period of religious dissension and disputes over political authority. In particular, Ali's accession was contested by Mu'awiya, the powerful governor of Syria and a relative of Othman. It led to the Battle of Siffin in Iraq (657); but the two sides decided to settle their dispute through arbitration. The arbitrators came to an interesting decision: they suggested that both sides should give up their claims and a new person should be elected caliph. Far from settling the dispute, the arbitration increased the enmity of the two sides and led to further dissent. A group of Ali's supporters felt that the caliphate was discredited and formed a party of their own, the Kharjites, or the seceders. They became the first sect to break way from the mainstream of Islam.

Ali was murdered in early 661 as he entered the mosque at Kufa for morning prayers. He was buried a few miles from Kufa. His burial site developed into the town of Najaf which became a centre for pilgrimage.

Kharjites

The lives of the rightly guided caliphs illustrate that the formative phase of Islam was not without turmoil. Indeed, three of the four caliphs were murdered. Most of the dissent focused on the question of succession: who had the right to political leadership of the Muslim community. One particular group of rebels, who were responsible for the murder of Ali, were known as the Kharjites. The Kharjites were a puritan sect who believed that there should be no debate or compromise on the question of succession: the 'decision is God's alone'. They were prone to extremist proclamations, denouncing Ali as well as Othman, and pronounced everyone who did not agree with their point of view as infidel and outside the law.

The Kharjites developed a radically different interpretation of what it means to be a Muslim. To be a Muslim, they argued, is to be in a perfect state of the soul. Someone in that state cannot commit a sin and engage in doing wrong. Sin, therefore, was a contradiction for a true Muslim – it nullified the believer and demonstrated that inwardly he was an apostate who had turned against Islam. Thus anyone who did any wrong was not really a Muslim and consequently could be put to death. Indeed, the Kharjites believed that all non-Kharjite Muslims were really apostates who were legitimate targets for violence.

There was, however, one point on which the Kharjite position was quite sensible. They objected to the caliphate becoming an Arab kingdom. Islam, they argued, was being infused with Arab chauvinism, and Arab tribal customs were becoming an integral part of the faith. They pointed to the practice of inducting non-Arab converts into tribes and appointing Arab 'protectors' over new non-Arab converts as signs of Arab supremacy. Indeed, they argued that non-Arabs were generally being relegated to an inferior status.

It was Caliph Ali who first attempted to suppress the Kharjite rebellion. Although they were heavily defeated, the Kharjites continued to be a source of insurrection against the caliphate for many centuries.

The formative history of Islam is not without its warts. But it does tell us how the Prophet himself and his closest companions lived their lives. It is these lives which are a constant source of inspiration for Muslims. By learning from and following these personal, human examples, Muslims try to give practical shape to what they believe.

4

What Do Muslims Believe?

As we saw in the previous chapter, the word 'Islam' has the dual meaning of 'peace' and 'submission'. A Muslim is one who 'submits' willingly to the guidance of one, all-knowing, all-powerful, merciful and beneficent God. This guidance is revealed in the Qur'an. It is given a practical shape in the Sunnah, the examples, actions and traditions of the Prophet Muhammad. Peace is sought within the parameters of eternal concepts and values furnished by the Qur'an and Sunnah.

Islam describes itself as *din*, a divine institution which guides rational beings, by their choosing it, to salvation in this world and the Hereafter. It covers both articles of belief and actions. In particular, din covers three things: *iman* or faith, *ihsan* or right actions, and the ritual expression of faith, what are known as 'Five Pillars' of Islam.

Iman or faith is the foundation of Islam. In Islam, faith is acquired both through rational exercise as well as through the experience of the Divine. We are born in a natural state of purity and grace. This state is called fitrah. Appreciation of the Divine is an integral part of our fitrah. Islam, therefore, sees itself as the natural way or tendency of human beings.

Submission to God thus leads to harmony. It is the realization of what is inherent in one's good and true nature. Iman is 'like a good tree whose root is firm and whose branches are high in the sky, yielding constant fruit by its Lord's leave'. (*Qur'an* 14:24–5)

Iman always goes hand in hand with Ihsan. Belief alone is not enough. One has to believe *and* do good. Believers are judged not by the proclamations of their beliefs but by their actions. Muslims believe that God has created humanity and the world not for sport or in vain – but for a purpose. And the purpose is this: that human beings may fulfil their natural ethical inclinations, do good and spread goodness on earth. So believers vie with each other to do better and better, greater and greater, and nobler and nobler deeds. The good life, in this world and the Hereafter, is a function of good deeds done here and now: 'To whoever, male or female, does good deed and has faith, We shall give a good life and reward them according to the best of their actions.' (*Qur'an* 16:97)

Articles of Faith

The basic constituents of iman are the six articles of faith. These articles are derived from the Qur'an; and at their foundation is the assumption that the Qur'an is the Word of God. Without this basic postulation – or cardinal belief – the articles of faith do not make much sense. However, they are very similar to the belief systems of other monotheistic faiths such as Judaism and Christianity. Not all of them play a role in the daily lives of Muslims – but most Muslims take their belief in God and the Day of Judgement very seriously.

1 God

The cornerstone of Muslim belief is the notion of *tawheed*, or the affirmation of the unity of God. The opposite of tawheed is partnership, the associating of gods with God, which is seen by Islam as the ultimate sin. God in Islam is beyond human imagination – even though we may use such terms as loving, speaking, being displeased when we speak about God – and human conception. To avoid any anthropomorphic conception of the Divine Being, the term Allah – always written with a capital A – is used. 'Allah' is a synthesis of two words: the definite article 'Al' and 'ilah', meaning Divinity. So the term itself incorporates the notion of one God. It reconstitutes in language a Reality that is beyond human imagination and perception. Through the word 'Allah', humans call upon God *personally*. It is the opening onto the Divine Essence, beyond language and the world.

The only way for humans to understand the Divine is through His attributes. The opening chapter of the Qur'an provides us with the four main attributes of God. Allah is the Lord (*Rabb*) who creates, maintains and brings all that is in the universe to a state of perfection. He is Beneficent (*al-Rahman*) and Merciful (*al-*Rahim), Whose love and mercy are manifested in the creation of this world. And He is the Master (*Malik*) of the Day of Judgement. The Qur'an begins:

> Praise be to Allah, the Lord of the Worlds,
> The Beneficent, the Merciful
> Master of the Day of Judgement
> It is You we worship;
> It is You we ask for help (1:1–4)

2 Angels

Muslims believe in angels who are purely spiritual beings, without any physical desires or material needs. Their food is to celebrate God's glory. Their drink is to proclaim his Majesty. Their pleasure is to worship Him. The angels are created with different forms and with different powers. Each is charged with a certain duty. The three main angels are: Jibril (Gabriel), the angel of revelation, Israfil, the angel who will announce the advent of the Day of Judgement, and Azrail, the angel of death. Angels, the Muslim tradition suggests, do not make themselves known to ordinary man – only to Prophets.

3 Books of God

Muslims believe that God has not left humanity without guidance. Throughout the ages, God sent His revelation through His books. So, for example, Moses received the Torah and Jesus the Gospels. These, and others, are seen as true revelations – all of which contain the same message: to worship One God and do good. However, according to Muslims, these revelations have been corrupted or not preserved in their original forms. Only the Qur'an, the last revelation from God, has been preserved in its original form. This does not stop Muslims from respecting the sacred sources of other faiths, or indeed following their commandments.

4 Prophets of God

Muslims believe that God sent His Messengers and prophets to every nation and community. The message of all prophets was the same. They all asked the people of their time to obey and worship Allah and none other. All messengers were mortals, endowed with Divine revelations and appointed by God to teach humanity. They were people of high calibre who always told the truth, committed no unlawful acts or concealed any part of the message they had to deliver. Although the Qur'an only mentions the Biblical Prophets (Adam, Noah, Lot, Abraham, Ishmael, Isaac, Jacob, Moses, David, Solomon, Yahya [John the Baptist], Jesus), Muslims believe that other nations, cultures and civilizations, such as India, China and Japan, also had their own prophets. Some Muslims have even argued that Plato and Aristotle, as well as Ram and Buddha, were prophets too. However, the Prophet Muhammad is seen as 'the Seal of the Prophets' and the last of the Messengers of God.

5 The Day of Judgement

Muslims believe that they will be accountable for all their thoughts and actions in this world on the Day of Judgement. On this day, the world will be rolled up as a scroll, and everyone will stand in judgement before God. Those with good deeds will be rewarded with Paradise. Others will spend time in Hell. The Muslim ideas of Heaven and Hell are purely metaphorical. The most frequently used term for paradise is 'garden'. 'Here,' says the Qur'an, 'is a picture of the Garden promised to the pious: rivers of water forever pure, rivers of milk forever fresh, rivers of wine, a delight for those who drink, rivers of honey clarified and pure, all flow in it; there they will find fruit of every kind, and they will find forgiveness from their Lord.' (47:15) In contrast, hell is frequently equated with fire, a place of torment. But these descriptions, as the Qur'an itself states, are just 'similitudes': the real nature of paradise and hell are known only to God.

Belief in the Day of Judgement means that death is not the end of life but a gateway to eternal life. As the Prophet Muhammad said, 'The grave is the first step of the journey to eternity.' Muslims thus see time as continuous from this world to the next; and time spent on this world will shape the nature of eternal time. This is why belief alone is not good enough; it has to be supplemented with good, just and charitable deeds. The account that one has to render on the Day of Judgement is a personal account – only one's own deeds, and not intercession by someone else, will lead to salvation.

Muslims have developed a fantastic eschatology around the Day of Judgement, the nature of paradise and hell. But much of this theology is folklore that can easily be dismissed as such.

6 Destiny

Muslims believe that their destiny is firmly in the hands of God. The outcome of every effort, every good intention and action is subject to the will of God. He is Wise, Loving and Just and has knowledge of past, present and future. What may appear to be a failure in the short run may turn out to be a great success in the long term. Therefore, setback, tragedies and hurdles in life should never lead to hopelessness. The believers must always have faith and trust in God. Their responsibility is to make sound choices and do their best. To plan and execute their plans with utmost diligence. But if things do not go well, they should not lose faith or give in to despair. Believers are always hopeful.

Apart from its theological significance, the term din also has a cultural dimension. There is an intimate connection between the concept of din and the idea of medina or city. We have seen that after the Prophet's migration from Mecca to Yathrib, the town changed its name to al-Medina – the city. Or more precisely, the *Medina-tun Nabi*: the City of the Prophet. It was here that the first community of believers lived freely by its din and built a civic society. The idea of din and civic society are intrinsically linked. Islam, therefore, sees itself not only as faith and religion, but also as culture and civilization. Ultimately,

Islam is a way of looking at and shaping the world, a system of knowing, being and doing, a process of building a civic society and a civilization. In short: a worldview. This is what Muslims learn from the Qur'an.

What Is the Qur'an?

Islam begins and ends with the Qur'an, the term literally means 'the Reading'. Muslims believe that the Qur'an is the Word of God. It is the written record of the Revelation made to Prophet Muhammad, in Arabic, over a 23-year period from AD 610 to 632. Since it was revealed, the Qur'an has remained exactly the same, not a word, comma or full stop has been changed. This 'inimitability' has been possible because of the special heightened nature of its language, the interconnecting nature of its style, and the way the words combine and lock with each other. The Qur'an is not so much like an epic poem, but more like a symphony where every note is fixed in its place. Remove or change a note and the text falls out of synch. This also makes the Qur'an very easy to memorize. Muslims throughout the world memorize it word for word in its entirety – and carry it 'in their hearts and minds'.

The Qur'an describes itself as a 'Book of Guidance', and addresses its message to all humanity. Essentially, the message of the Qur'an is focused on the nature and ends of religious life, the 'what' of Divine will. There are some legislative verses, but these are few and limited. Out of a total of 6,342 verses (arranged in 114 chapters), hardly 500 are prescriptive. A great deal of the Qur'an is devoted to exploring the attributes of God and describing the quality of a just and righteous life. Around one-third of the Qur'an is devoted to extolling the virtues of reason.

The essence of the Qur'an's message is that God does not need to send another revelation. Partly because He has placed in human hands an imperishable and definitive statement of His will – the Qur'an itself. And partly because He wishes people to discover and to elaborate the means by which His will is to be understood and realized for themselves. Thus, it is not just revelation that directs and shapes human behaviour but also reason, reflection, philosophy, science and the study of the material world. The Qur'an gives equal importance to both revelation and reason as signposts and guides to human behaviour. It is thus not an accident that the Qur'an is not very prescriptive. Instead, it constantly asks questions – have you not looked around you and studied the cosmos, have you not looked into the history of other nations, have you not travelled on the earth to explore its flora and fauna? – and urges the believers to engage with the material world. It places the burden of law-making on human beings themselves. But in all cases it emphasizes that religious ethics should play a part in shaping a society. For quite some time, I believe, Muslims have overlooked the other side of the equation and concentrated solely on revelation – much to the detriment of Muslim societies.

The major themes of the Qur'an include the unity of God, human beings as individuals and communities, nature and environment, revelation, life after death and the nature of evil. The Qur'an also focuses on events in the life of the Prophet Muhammad, the circumstance of the Muslim community in Mecca, the emergence of the civic society in Medina, and the history of earlier civilizations.

These themes and subjects are not delineated in a single place. They occur, and re-occur, in a number of places throughout the text. Like the Bible, the Qur'an is not structured as a linear narrative. Neither are its verses arranged in chronological order according the sequence in which they were revealed. Instead, the arrangement takes the reader from the issues of 'what' and 'how' to the ultimate question: 'why'. Throughout, the Qur'an uses metaphors, allegories and parables to delineate its themes and subjects, returning to the same topics again and again. The repetition adds layers of significance, appends multiple meanings, and constantly expands the boundaries of possible interpretation. The Qur'an thus makes sense as an interconnected, interlaced text with a host of possible meanings.

The ultimate goal of a Muslim life is to engage with the text of the Qur'an and interpret, reinterpret and decipher its multiple layers of meaning. It is a text revealed in history. The Qur'an, therefore, has to be interpreted within its context. It is also a commentary on the life of the Prophet Muhammad. Muhammad, the recipient of the revelation, is thus the ultimate guide to its interpretation and understanding. So, in the first instance, the verses of the Qur'an have to be seen in specific historical context. However, the Qur'an is not a narrative history. It is a commentary on the meaning and implication of history, including the personal history of the Prophet Muhammad himself. Thus the context may be specific – but its implications are universal and eternal.

What this means is that the Qur'an cannot be interpreted out of context. It has to be read in conjunction with the life of the Prophet, on which it is a commentary. We cannot lift individual verses from the Qur'an and use them to justify things without any reference to the context in which those verses were revealed. Neither can we interpret individual verses without reference to the rest of the Qur'an. This, I must admit, is a common practice amongst Muslims. And it has led to the literalist, atomistic and one-dimensional interpretations that have been used to justify all variety of unjust, patriarchal, chauvinist and violent actions – positions that are clearly contrary to the spirit of the holy text.

A faith community can only have an interpretative relationship with its sacred text. And that interpretation cannot be undertaken once and for all. Each generation of believers must reinterpret the text in the light of its own experience. This is what the Qur'an demands. And this is what Muslims have most conspicuously failed to do. Believers may not just disagree with the interpretations of previous generations. They may, ultimately, disagree between themselves. The Qur'an is not only open to multiple interpretations; it positively invites them.

However they may interpret their sacred texts, all Muslims make a clear distinction between the Qur'an and the Prophet. The Qur'an is the uncreated Word of God. But Muhammad is unquestionably human. This human life provides us with the best means of understanding the purpose and intentions of the sacred text. After the Qur'an, Muslims seek guidance from the Sunnah – the examples and actions of the Prophet Muhammad.

What Is the Sunnah?

Prophet Muhammad is not just the Messenger of God who conveyed His message to humanity. He is also the person who concretized and realized the Divine message in a particular situation. This is why the Qur'an declares Muhammad's conduct is an ideal example for Muslims to follow and emulate.

The Sunnah is divided into two categories: what the Prophet did and what the Prophet said.

In their daily lives, Muslims are supposed to follow what the Prophet did. So Muslims pray the way the Prophet prayed, perform their ablutions as he did, enact the rituals of the hajj (the pilgrimage to Mecca) by imitating his actions. And they should relate to their family, neighbourhood, society and others by following the Sunnah. But this is not always the case. The truth is that Muslims have made a fetish of the Prophet's appearance and forgotten his personality and actions.

So most devout Muslim men have a beard, dress as the Prophet is supposed to have dressed, eat with their hands, and clean their teeth with a *muswak* – a chewing stick with anti-bacterial properties. But the Prophet's generosity and forgiveness, compassion and civility, his strong sense of justice and equality, his passion for thought and learning are often conspicuous by their absence. It is far easier to demonstrate piety by imitating the superficial and ignoring the deep and enduring.

What the Prophet said has evolved into a sophisticated discipline in its own right. Muslims make a clear distinction between the words of the Qur'an and the words of the Prophet. The language, the style, the structure of the two are quite distinct. And unlike the Qur'an which is preserved by Divine will, the words of the Prophet had to be preserved by human effort. Thus identifying the authentic sayings of the Prophet, called *hadith*, became a major challenge for Muslims, a challenge met by the early Muslim communities with formidable intellectual acumen and scrupulous care.

An entire science evolved out of the project to collect, shift through, edit and compile authentic hadith. The task had two dimensions.

First, the actual sayings of the Prophet had to be collected. This required collectors of hadith to travel far and wide throughout the Muslim world seeking individuals who had direct contact with either the Prophet or one of his trusted companions. A technique was involved which placed the narrators in a chain, stretching from the person relating the hadith right back to the Prophet himself. The narrators in the chain had to be in a position to have met physically, their conduct had to be impeccably moral, and what they had to report had to be verifiable. Hadith collectors observed these conditions meticulously.

On one particular occasion, the famous scholar Imam Bukhari (810–70) travelled several hundred miles to meet a person who was in possession of a single hadith. When he arrived at the man's house, he found the person beckoning his horse with an empty bag of fodder. Bukhari returned without talking to the man. How could he be trusted, he declared, to convey a hadith when he was deceitful to his horse?

Muslims developed such disciplines as biography, historiography and social analysis to investigate the truthfulness of the narrators of the hadith. Only when the narrators had been thoroughly checked, and their integrity established beyond doubt, would a hadith be recorded. This is why the hadith often have the form: 'So and so said that so and so said that the Prophet said . . .'

Second, the text of the hadith had to be examined critically. Its language had to be the language of the Prophet. The content had to be coherent. It had to be rational. It had to correspond with the teachings of the Qur'an. And it had to conform to historical reality and with the accumulated wisdom of humanity.

Elaborate tools for textual analysis were developed. Using grammar, syntax, lexicography, etymology, philology and literary aesthetics, the compilers of hadith examined the form and content of each one. On the basis of this criticism, hadith were classified as:

1 *sahih* or authentic, related by narrators of unimpeachable integrity;

2 *hasan* or good, but with one weak link in the chain of narrators;

3 *daeef* or weak, with a defective chain of narrators.

There are numerous other types of hadith: for example, hadith which had one missing narrator at the beginning (suspended) or towards the end of the chain (defective); or where the narrators are accused of falsehood (discarded) or where the narrators have made a mistake in language (denounced), or where the saying is in contradiction to what the prophet said elsewhere or what the Qur'an says (contradictory).

The hadith that really matter are the authentic ones. Out of the millions which were collected, only a couple of thousand are considered authentic. These are collected in six canonical collections of which two are acknowledged to be the most important: *Sahih Bukhari* of Imam Bukhari and *Sahih Muslim* of Imam Muslim.

Imam Bukhari and Imam Muslim are regarded as the greatest compilers of hadith.

Imam Bukhari, as his name suggests, was born in Bukhara and was renowned for his intellect and retentive memory. He travelled hundreds of miles to collect, check and recheck the authenticity of hadith. He is said to have collected 600,000 sayings of the Prophet. But after examination, he reduced them to 7,275 which he thought to be reliable. Further scrupulous scholarship reduced them to 2,762 which he described as 'authentic'.

Imam Muslim, who was born in Khurasan, was just as critical. He collected over three million sayings, but included only 9,200 in his book.

The hadith have become the main source of the Prophet's Sunnah. Indeed, the two words – hadith and Sunnah – have become synonymous. To follow the Sunnah has essentially become a matter of following certain sayings of the Prophet. This in itself is not problematic. But there are sectarian differences of opinion about the traditions, which were collected over several decades a hundred years after the death of the Prophet. The Shia Muslims, for example, tend to reject the Sunni books and rely on their own collections. Moreover, inauthentic traditions are also used by some Muslims to justify their positions. So different sayings of the Prophet, including unreliable ones, can be used to emphasize different aspects of Islam, and take the believers in different directions, even leading to sectarian violence.

There is another aspect of the sayings of the Prophet that is not widely appreciated by the Muslims. The Prophet was a man of his time. Whatever he said, with all his foresight, is grounded in the context of his period. So not everything he said or did can be universalized or turned into a general principle. He dressed and went about his business according to the dictates of his time and environment. But many of his sayings, such as 'learn to know yourself' and 'strive always to excel in virtue and truth', have universal import. What is important is to look at the spirit, the underlying values, of his words and actions.

The Qur'an and the Sunnah, the Muslims believe, establish the divinely ordained pattern of human conduct. The purpose of a Muslim life is to realize this pattern in individual lives as well as in society at large. This is where the Shariah comes in.

What Is the Shariah?

Literally, the word 'Shariah' means 'the path leading to water'. In a more general sense, it has meant 'the highway to a good life'. Religiously, it has come to be equated with 'Islamic Law'.

The Shariah is said to be *derived* from the Qur'an and the Sunnah. It is the way ordained by God. To conduct one's life according to the dictates of the Shariah is thus to realize the Divine Will. Not surprisingly, most Muslims believe that the Shariah itself is divine.

The Shariah is a highly practical concept, concerned largely with human conduct. But it has a very holistic perspective on human behaviour. It includes spiritual, mental, physical, social, and institutional aspects of human conduct. As such, the Shariah is both faith and practice. How Muslims pray and how they pay their zakat is just as much part of the Shariah as how Muslims should marry and divorce, or how thieves and robbers should be punished. The Shariah aims to be comprehensive. It represents a total way of life.

But how are we to know the Shariah?

Right from the inception of Islam, two methods of 'knowing' the Shariah were recognized. The first was simple. It required the exegesis of the Qur'an and the Sunnah. But these traditional sources could not suffice for a rapidly developing community. So a second principle was established: the use of reason and human intelligence to 'understand' or 'comprehend' the Divine Will.

The use of independent reasoning to elaborate and under-stand the Shariah was sanctioned by the Prophet Muhammad himself. According to an authentic tradition, the Prophet sent a certain Muadh ibn Jabal to Yemen as a governor. Before he left to take up his appointment, the Prophet asked ibn Jabal how he would judge matters when confronted with a problem. Ibn Jabal replied he would judge on the basis of the Qur'an. The Prophet asked him: 'Assuming that you do not find it in the Qur'an, on what basis would you judge?' Ibn Jabal replied he would judge on the basis of the Sunnah. The Prophet asked him again: 'Assuming that you do not find it in both the Qur'an and the Sunnah, on what basis would you judge?' 'Then,' ibn Jabal replied, 'I would judge on the basis of my own independent reasoning.' The Prophet is said to have been very happy with the reply.

Independent reasoning, or *ijtihad*, became the cornerstone for understanding the Shariah, and developed into a major principle of Islam. Indeed, it is the central principle for adjusting to change within Islam.

A string of other secondary sources also emerged to develop the understanding of the Shariah. The two main ones are *ijma* and *qiyas*. Ijma means 'consensus'; originally, it meant the consensus of the Muslim community. Historically, the term came to mean 'the consensus of the learned jurists'. Qiyas is analogical deduction; it is a particular form of ijtihad. It involves drawing parallels from the Qur'an and the Sunnah between two different situations. Legal judgements reached by analogy become part of Islamic law if they acquire the ijma of the Muslim jurists.

Later on, supplementary sources were added to refine interpretations of the Shariah. These included:

1   *al-Istihsan*, or the deviation, on a certain issue, from the rule of precedent to another rule for a more relevant legal reason that requires such deviation.
2   *al-Istislah*, or public interest that necessitates certain rulings not specifically sanctioned by the Qur'an or the Sunnah.
3   *al-Urf*, or the custom and practice of a particular society that does not violate the general principle of the Qur'an and the Sunnah.

What Muslims now know as the Shariah is in fact the cumulative effort to understand the Divine Will using these sources and methods. The Islamic term for 'understanding' is *fiqh*, which also has the technical meaning of 'jurisprudence'. So the bulk of the Shariah is fiqh or jurisprudence developed during the classical period, from the seventh to the tenth century. It is a law that developed in a specific historic context with a particular understanding of the world.

Those who framed Islamic law have the honorific title of Imam, or leader whose example is to be followed. The Sunni majority branch of Islam recognizes four legal Schools of Thought, each carrying the name of their founders.

Imam Abu Hanifa (d. 772) was the first to establish his school. It is said that he took thirty years to codify his laws. His constant refusal to accept the post of chief justice eventually led to his imprisonment in Baghdad, where he died. Imam Malik (d. 801), who was born and died in Medina, is the author of the renowned book *Muwatta*, 'the way made smooth'. It is considered as the first great corpus of Islamic law. Imam Shafi'i (d. 820) was the first to write a treatise on the principle of Islamic jurisprudence. He was a disciple of Imam Malik, but differed from his teacher in emphasizing moderation and temperance. Imam Hanbal (d. 855) was a disciple of Imam Shafi'i. He lived the life of an ascetic, and was persecuted for his outspoken opinions.

There are several schools of law in the Shia minority branch of Islam. The most important is the Jafari, named after Ja'far as-Sadiq (699–765), who was the teacher of both Malik ibn Abas and Abu Hanifa.

Different parts of the Muslim world subscribe to different legal schools. The Hanafi school is dominant in Turkey, India and Pakistan. The Malaki school has most of its followers in the Middle East and West Africa. The Shafi'i school is popular in Southeast Asia. The Hanbali school is followed in Saudi Arabia and Qatar. The Jafari school predominates in Iran and Iraq.

The classical jurists did not set out to establish schools of law. Neither did they consider their own juristic opinions and judgements to be infallible, eternal and set in stone. They were all very humble men aware of their own shortcomings. What they set out to do was to establish the principle that a Muslim society should operate within moral and ethical limits, and that critical judgement and independent reasoning should rule the day. They refused to cooperate with the rulers and openly fought against tyranny and despotism. They constantly emphasized that their opinions were just that – opinions.

But over time Muslims have made these opinions, developed in and applicable largely to a medieval world, totally sacrosanct. On the whole they cannot be challenged, changed or abandoned. Over the centuries, these opinions became an integral part of the Shariah, which is supposed to be divine and immutable; they are thus deeply entrenched. To question these opinions is tantamount to questioning the Shariah, something that most pious Muslims abhor. Thus a law that was supposed to be dynamic and progressive has been frozen in history. What was a human construction in history, an attempt to understand the Divine Will in a particular context, is now seen as immutable. What this means is that when Muslim countries adopt the Shariah in contemporary times they reproduce the medieval context in full – complete with its division of the world between believers and unbelievers, patriarchal notions, tenth-century criminal law and puritanical outlook. This is why Muslim states, such as Saudi Arabia and Sudan, which have instituted Shariah law with archaic crime and punishment laws and antiquated notions of women's rights, have such a medieval feel. Ironically, what was originally devised to fight tyranny has become a source of tyranny itself.

All Muslims believe in the articles of faith, the Qur'an, the Sunnah and the Shariah. But different types of Muslim have somewhat different beliefs.

5

Varieties of Muslim Belief

There are distinct differences between the belief systems of the two major groups in Islam – the Sunnis and Shia. As the majority community, most beliefs we associate with Islam are Sunni beliefs. The Sufis also have a few beliefs that are particular to them. And beyond that different groups of Muslims, such as puritans and moderates, emphasize different aspects of Islam.

Shia

The Shia Muslims, unlike the Sunnis, believe in hereditary spiritual leadership. They insist that only members of the Prophet's family have the right to be leaders. Consequently, they believe that the Prophet should have been succeeded by Ali, his cousin and son-in-law. Thus, in Shiaism Ali has a special place and function.

The Shia argue that the Prophet himself choose Ali as his successor. In one particular event at Ghadir Khumm, the Prophet is said to have chosen Ali for the 'general guardianship' of the Muslim community. This claim is based on a number of hadith which the Sunni Muslims do not accept as authentic.

The hereditary leadership is known as the Imamate. The Imams possess extraordinary grace, miraculous power and special (secret) knowledge. Ali was the first Imam and is even mentioned in the Shia call to prayer (azan) – much to the dismay of the Sunnis. The central event of Shia theology is the battle of Karbala.

We have seen that Caliph Ali's accession was contested by Muawiya, the founder of the Umayyad dynasty. Ma'awiya was succeeded by his son, Yazid. The Muslim community split between those who supported Ali and those who supported Yazid. After Ali, his supporters gathered around his son, Hussain, the grandson of the Prophet. Hussain launched an alternative bid for the leadership of the Muslim community.

On 10 October 680, Hussain and his followers faced the army of Yazid. Hereditary monarchy was challenged by spiritual heredity. The battle took place at Karbala, on the west bank of the Euphrates. Hussain and his six hundred followers had no chance. But they refused to surrender. A massacre followed; and Islam was split in two for ever.

The events of Karbala are re-enacted every year on the tenth day of the Islamic month of Muharram. It is a day of mourning and remembering the plight of Hussain. Ta'iziyyah, or Shia martyrdom plays, are performed. Processions are led through the streets. Men and women beat their chests, and men flagellate themselves with knives and chains; it is an expression of guilt for having abandoned Hussain in his hour of need. The Shia also go to Karbala on pilgrimage. As a constant reminder of the events of Karbala, they prostrate their heads, when they pray, on a round tablet of Karbala clay.

The Shias have developed their own schools of law, elaborate philosophies and mystical traditions. There are numerous subdivisions within Shiaism. All believe in the infallibility of the

Imams, but different sects believe in a different number of Imams. The dominant sect is the 'Twelver' Shias, who believe in a dozen Imams, starting with Ali and Hussain. The twelfth Imam, Imam Mahdi, was born in Samarra, the only child of Hasan al-Askari, the eleventh Imam. After the death of al-Askari in 873, Imam Mahdi, then aged four, disappeared. Shia theology postulates that he has been living supernaturally hidden from humanity, and will reveal himself at the end of time. In his absence, a Shia scholar, an Ayatollah, can act as his 'shadow'. Ayatollah Khomeini, the leader of the Iranian revolution, was said to be *Vilat-e-faqih* – the shadow of the missing Imam. As such, his judgements and *fatwas* (opinions) were seen by the devout as infallible.

Other Shia sects include the Zaydis, who accept five Imams. The Ismailis Shia, who recognize seven Imams, are led by the Aga Khan.

Sufis

The Sufis represent the mystical tendency in Islam. Unlike most Muslims, who believe that proximity to God can only be achieved after death, the Sufis believe that it is possible to experience the closeness of God while one is alive. To achieve this closeness, one must undertake a journey, known as *tariqas* (literally, 'the path'), under the supervision of a spiritual guide. The journey requires extra prayers, known as *zikr* (remembrance of God). Sufis also believe in the 'unity of truth', arguing that all spiritual paths lead to one and the same God.

Sufism emerged early in Islam as a reaction against puritanism and arid legalism and established itself as a movement with Hasan al-Basri (d. 728). He was brought up by Umm Salama, one of the wives of the Prophet. Muslims should seek 'sweetness', he declared, in prayer, in remembering God and in reading the Qur'an.

The first recognized mystic of Islam is Rabia al-Basri, whose life is shrouded in mystery. We know that she was a freed slave, who retreated to the desert where she lived a life of poverty. She rejected numerous offers of marriage, but accepted Hasan al-Basri as a student. She is renowned for her mystical poetry, some of which is still widely available. Rabia al-Basri is credited with the notion of unconditional love, which is captured in her famous prayer: 'O God, if I worship you for the fear of hell, burn me in hell. If I worship you in hope of paradise, exclude me from paradise. But if I worship you for your own sake, grudge me not Your everlasting Beauty.'

The purpose of Sufis life is to seek *fana*, or the annihilation of the ego. The first step to fana is abandonment of materialism. The term Sufi comes from the word *suf*, meaning 'wool'. The Sufis wore robes made of undyed wool as a symbol of their renunciation of the world and its pleasures. The most celebrated incident of reaching the state of fana is attributed to al-Hallaj (d. 922). In a state of ecstasy, al-Hallaj uttered the words, 'I am the Truth.' This led to problems with religious authorities. Al-Hallaj refused to apologize; indeed, he repeated the performance on a number of occasions. Eventually, at his own insistence, he was executed.

Muslim history is full of great Sufi mystics. The Andalusian, ibn Arabi (d. 1240), is considered one of the greatest of all time. The Turkish Sufi, Jalal-al-Din Rumi (d. 1273), comes a close second. Such illustrious Sufis established their own tariqas which their disciples follow to this day.

Sufism has also been a great stimulus to poetry and literature. The *Mathnavi* of Rumi, full of parables and stories, is widely read by Muslims everywhere. Great Persian and Urdu poetry stem from Sufism as can be seen in the works of Umar Khayyam (d. 1124), Sadi (d. 1292), Hafiz (d. 1390) and more recently, Mohammad Iqbal (d. 1938).

Puritans and Reformers

Besides these broad divisions, there are also differences of perception that have direct bearing on belief. The puritans, for example, believe that Islam should not admit any change. It should be practised, implemented, indeed imposed, on society in exactly the same way that it existed in during its formative phase. The puritan term for change is bida (literally, innovation). They see bida not just as bad but as something that is forbidden.

Radical fundamentalists equate Islam with the state. What is fundamental about fundamentalist belief is that Islam and state are one and the same thing. Thus, they seek to establish 'Islamic states' ruled by Islamic Law and religious scholars. Fundamentalists also believe that the West, in general, and the USA, in particular, is intrinsically inimical to Islam. In the words of the Ayatollah Khomeini, the USA is the 'Great Satan'.

Ironically, the fundamentalists of today are the heirs of the reformists of the last few centuries. One of the first reformers was Muhammad bin Abdul Wahhab (1703–87), who established the Wahhabi brand of Islam. Abd al-Wahhab was a puritan and argued against all forms of innovation in Islam. He wanted Islam to return to the purity of the time of the Prophet and the rightly guided caliphs; and he insisted on the strict observance of religious duties as he saw them. Many fundamentalists are Wahhabis.

However, not all reformers are puritans. In India, Abd al-Wahhab's contemporary, Shah Waliullah (1703–63), sought a different route to reform. He was a Sufi and promoted a more spiritual interpretation of Islam. He combined his mysticism with social justice and believed that the entire system of Islam needed to be rethought in a spirit of inquiry. The followers of this tradition could now be describe as 'liberals'.

The belief that Islam needs to be reformed politically, socially and culturally, as I noted earlier, has existed since pre-colonial times. A number of reform movements began with overtly political and social goals. In Sudan, Muhammad ibn Sayyid Abd Allah (1844–85), better known as the *Mahdi* of Sudan, led a rebellion against the British. Sayyid Muhammad bin Ali as-Sanusi (1791–1859) founded the Sanusi movement in Libya. He preached an eclectic mix of Wahhabi puritanism and eso-teric Sufi thought and spearheaded resistance to European expansion. In Nigeria, Usman dan Fodio (d. 1817) led a reform movement noted for its liberalism and emphasis on social jus-tice. He established the Sokoto Caliphate, which became the backbone of resistance against the British and the French.

At the beginning of the twentieth century, reformist move-ments acquired an international dimension. The emphasis now shifted to 'pan-Islamic' reform – meaning social, economic, cultural, intellectual as well as religious reform throughout the Muslim world. The leading light was Jamal al-Din al-Afghani (1838–97), an intellectual who believed that Muslims should engage with modernity and learn from the West. He joined forces with Muhammad Abduh (1849–1905), the Mufti of Egypt. Together they published an intellectual magazine, *Al-Urwa Al-Wuthqa* (The Firm Bond), which became highly influential in the Arab world.

During the second half of the twentieth century, the reformist agenda was dominated by two mass organizations: the Muslim Brotherhood of Egypt and Jamaat-e-Islami of Pakistan. Syed Qutb (1906–66), the chief ideologue of the Brotherhood, was imprisoned, tortured and finally executed by the regime of Jamal Abdel Nasser. Towards the end of his life, he came to believe that armed revolt against the state was a necessity. Abu Ala Maududi (1903–79), the founder of the Jamaat, favoured democracy as a route to establishing an 'Islamic state'. Both Qutb and Maududi believed in the importance of unchanging tradition and offered a puritan interpretation of Islam.

During the second half of the twentieth century, Jamaat-e-Islami and the Muslim Brotherhood became the backbone of what came to be known as the 'Islamic movement'. These organizations had a tremendous influence on politically orientated Muslims throughout the world – from Sudan and Egypt to Bangladesh and Indonesia, as well as Muslim minorities in Europe and America. The Islamic movement worked to create 'Islamic states', where religion and the state were one and the same thing under the general rubric of Shariah law. Jamaat-e-Islami worked relentlessly to transform Pakistan and Bangladesh into 'Islamic states', while the Muslim Brotherhood sought similar transformations in Egypt, Sudan and other parts of the Middle East. While the majority who subscribed to the goals of the Islamic movement were content to fight their battles by democratic means, a small minority opted for violence. Most radical Muslim groups have been inspired, one way or another, by the Islamic movement.

But the puritans and followers of 'Islamic movement' are a diminishing minority. Most Muslims believe that Islam is an open system, that pluralism and diversity are intrinsic to Islam, that Islam is the 'middle path' which shuns all kinds of fanaticism and extremism. This is the silent, moderate majority.

All varieties of Muslims – Sunnis, Shias, Sufis, puritans as well as moderates – have to fulfil certain duties of their faith throughout their lives.

6

What Do Muslims Do?

All Muslims have four obligations: to offer the daily prayers, fast during the Islamic month of Ramadan, pay a regular amount of their income for the poor and the needy, and perform the pilgrimage to Mecca at least once in their lifetime if they can afford to do so. Collectively, these duties are often referred to as 'the pillars of Islam'.

Prayer

Prayer has a very important significance in Islam. It is both the first step towards a spiritual life and the highest level of spiritual perfection. It is both a means of levelling differences (of rank, class, colour and nationality) and a method for acquiring humility, love, moral rectitude and human solidarity. The technical term for prayer is *salah*. It denotes an ensemble of inner and outer actions carried out when prayer is performed. It includes the ablutions, the intention of reciting the prayer, the request for grace and pardon, the recitation of the verses from the Qur'an and the appropriate physical movements.

The object of the form that prayer takes in Islam is to concentrate attention on a single goal: the realization of the Divine presence. The standing position with which the prayer starts, the bowing down, the kneeling with the forehead placed on the ground, and the reverent sitting posture – all help to realize the Divine presence as a fact. Throughout the entire prayer, the worshipper is focused and does not turn his or her attention to anything else. The salah is thus an undisturbed meditation on the Divine. It is for this reason that prayer in Islam is accompanied not with music but with the recitation of the Qur'an, the Divine Words themselves.

According to the practice of the Prophet, prayer is performed five times a day at specific times:

1 *fajr*, the early morning prayer, performed after dawn and before sunrise.
2 *zuhr*, the early afternoon prayer, performed after midday until late afternoon.
3 *asr*, the late afternoon prayer, performed late afternoon until just before sunset.
4 *maghrib*, the sunset prayer, performed immediately after the sun sets.
5 *isha*, the night prayer, performed until midnight or dawn.

Each prayer has two components: the obligatory part (*fard*) which ought to be said in congregation, preferably in a mosque; and the individual part (sunnah) which is said alone, even in a mosque. In congregation, the worshippers follow the lead of the Imam – who can be anyone – who selects the portions of the Qur'an to be recited. The congregation emphasizes both communion of man with God as well as the spiritual union and solidarity of man with man. During private prayer, the individual selects the verses of the Qur'an he or she wishes to recite. Thus, through prayer Muslims constantly refresh their faith and seek to live an enriched spiritual life.

Fasting

While prayer is a daily affair, fasting during the month of Ramadan is an annual ritual.

Fasting is a sublime spiritual exercise. In Islam, fasting is not an act of penitence but an exercise in self-reassurance and self-control. Its primary function is to instil spiritual discipline, develop an appreciation of the physical pains of hunger, and shape a realization for the maintenance of human dignity. Fasting is a form of travel; and those who fast, travel to attain proximity to God.

Fasting has a personal and social dimension. It teaches the individual to be prepared to suffer deprivation and undergo hardship rather than give into temptation. This lesson is repeated day after day for a whole month. Just as physical exercise strengthens the body, so moral exercise through fasting fortifies the resolve. The person who is able to control his or her desire is the person who can attain true spiritual and moral greatness. A fasting person is not only required to abstain from food, drink and sex, but to avoid all immoral thoughts and actions.

Socially, the rich and poor are brought to the same level; in their private existence, both go through the same hardship. And both are required to go out during the month of Ramadan to do good to humanity. In Islamic tradition, the doors of heaven are opened during Ramadan, the month in which the Qur'an was revealed. Hence, throughout the month, Muslims offer extra prayers and the entire Qur'an is recited from cover to cover.

It is worth noting that the Islamic calendar is lunar. The months of the Hijra calendar are determined by the positions of the moon, each month being twenty-nine or thirty days in length. The Muslim year is thus shorter than the Gregorian year by about eleven days. This means that the month of Ramadan may occur in different seasons. Over a cycle of thirty-three years, Islamic months take a complete turn and fall during the same season. Thus the advantages or disadvantages of fasting during a particular season are distributed equally over the entire Muslim world.

MONTHS OF THE MUSLIM CALENDAR

Muharram

Safar

Rabee' al-Awwal

Rabee' al-Thani

Jumanda al-Oola

Jumanda al-Thaniyah

Rajab

Sha'ban

Ramadan

Shawwal

Dhul-Qa'dah

Dhul-Hijjah

Zakat

It is usually during the month of Ramadan that Muslims pay their obligatory annual 'poor tax' or *zakat*. The word 'zakat' has the connotation of growth and purification. By giving zakat, Muslims purify their income and earnings; and plant a seed for the growth of their wealth. Zakat is not 'charity' in the sense that it is given to the poor because the poor have asked for it. It is given because the poor and the needy have a *right* to receive something from the more fortunate.

Muslims are urged to give as much in charity or *sadaqah* as they can and when they can. It is a matter of conscience; and they may choose not to give. But zakat is not a matter of conscience – it cannot be escaped. It is a duty and an obligation which must be fulfilled. Islam insists that wealth must not only be acquired through moral and legitimate means, but must also be shared with others. The Qur'an describes zakat as the essence of religion. In a small chapter entitled 'Common Kindness', the Qur'an asks: 'Who is the denier of religion itself?' The answer: 'It is he who pushes aside the orphans and does not urge others to feed the needy. So woe to those who pray but are heedless of their prayers, those who are all show and forbid common kindness.' (107:1–7)

Normally, zakat is paid at the rate of 2.5 per cent. As it is a tax on one's income and wealth, it is paid on all liquid and fixed assets, including property, jewellery, saving accounts, shares, bonds or agricultural produce. It matters little whether the owner is an adult or a minor, male or female, or even dead or alive. The trust or estate a person leaves behind is required to pay zakat even before any creditors' claims against it can be entertained. But zakat is not an indiscriminate tax. It is not levied on anything intended for consumption, or on a loss-making business. In the final analysis, zakat is an act of worship, and an exercise in spiritual fulfilment.

Hajj

Hajj, or pilgrimage to Mecca, is the fourth obligation of a Muslim. At least once in their lifetime, those with the financial means to do so must perform the hajj. The sacred journey to Mecca is taken during the twelfth month – Dhul Hijjah – of the Islamic calendar; and the hajj itself is performed during the eighth to the thirteenth of the month.

The word 'hajj' means 'effort'; and the pilgrimage requires both physical and spiritual effort. Normally, people go for hajj during the later years of their life. But my experience suggests that the best time to go on hajj is when one is in one's prime. For the hajj requires a great deal of walking, running, standing up, sleeping rough and coping with a general state of confusion. All of which is directed towards losing oneself in God, in overcoming one's ego, in forgetting one's self to a point where one surrenders completely to God both in the active hours of the day and in the hours of rest and quietness. This is why the hajj is considered to be the 'supreme effort' of a lifetime.

The hajj begins with the donning of the ihram: two sheets of unsewn white cloth for men, and a simple white dress for women. The ihram brings the pilgrims into a state of grace: from now on, they must not hurt or abuse anyone, not even an insect; do anything dishonest or arrogant; wear perfume or jewellery or engage in sex – the only thing they can do is to pray. And they pray constantly:

> What is Your command? I am here, O God.
> What is Your command? I am here, O God.
> You have no partner, here I am.
> Surely, praise and blessings are Yours, and Dominion.
> You have no partner.

Once in the state of ihram, the pilgrims make their way to the Ka'bah in the Sacred Mosque in Mecca. Visiting the Ka'bah is a profound, awe-inspiring experience for any Muslim. Even though I have visited the Ka'bah numerous times, it always generates the same feelings in me: excitement, fear and trembling, reverence and humility. Physically, the Ka'bah itself is not very imposing: it is a cube-like structure draped with a black cloth. But it is its symbolic significance that inspires devotees. It is the prime focus of the Muslim world, the direction that Muslims face when they pray. It is a symbol of Muslim unity and solidarity. But above all the Ka'bah is a Muslim's direct connection to the beginning of Islam and the life of the Prophet Muhammad. Thus, the Ka'bah is not just a physical location and a physical structure: it is the Beginning, the Past, the Present, and For ever of a Muslim. Whoever stands in front of the Ka'bah feels this and is shaken by the experience.

The pilgrims perform the ritual circumambulation of the Ka'bah seven times. And they pray:

O God, truly I seek refuge in You.
From doubt, and idolatry, and discord,
And hypocrisy and immorality,
And the evil eye.
And the perversion that is the worship
Of worldly things:
Wealth, family or offspring.

O God, truly I ask that You are pleased
With me, and grant me paradise.
And I take refuge in You.
From Your displeasure and the Fire.

O God, truly I seek refuge in You.
From the examination in the grave.
And I take refuge in You
From the trials of life
And death.

After the circumambulations, the pilgrims begin a series of rituals based on movements. The focus of attention in the Ka'bah is God. Now, the centre of drama shifts to humans. The pilgrims move to another part of the Sacred Mosque to run seven times between the small hills of Safa and Marwah. The hills, about five hundred metres apart, are joined by a long, marble-lined corridor. The pilgrims walk briskly between the hills, re-enacting the desperate search for water by the Prophet Ibrahim's wife, Hagar. It signifies the human soul's perpetual quest for the essence of spiritual tranquillity.

From the Sacred Mosque the pilgrims travel a few kilometres to the valley of Muna where they spend the night of the eighth day of Dhul-Hijjah. The following morning they enter the plains of Arafat. It is here that the pilgrims spend the supreme hours of hajj. Just as the sun passes the meridian, two million pilgrims stand in unison, and pray as they have never prayed before. From north to south, and east to west, as far as the eye can see, line after line of pilgrims, of all races, colours and class, all dressed in white, stand together, bow down in synch, and prostrate themselves in unison. They move and pray as one congregation. But the overall experience is individual. It is me and my God, face to face. And I address my God as though He were in front me, simply and directly. 'You,' I begin:

Rescuers of the drowned!
Saviour of the lost!

Witness of every secret thought!

End of all lamentations!

You, Whose beneficence is without beginning or end!

You, Whose goodness is eternal!

You, of Whom all things are in need!

And without Whom none can exist!

You, O God, Who provides provision for all –

And to Whom all return!

You, to Whom the hands of those who supplicate are lifted,

And towards Whom worshippers yearn!

I ask You to place us in Your protection,

And Your generosity,

And Your refuge,

And Your shelter,

And Your security.

The pilgrims stay at Arafat till sunset. Soon afterwards, begins the mass exodus to the parched fields of Muzdalifah. Here the pilgrims spend the night under the open sky. The following morning they make their way back to Muna. During their three-day stay in Muna, the pilgrims symbolically stone the 'Devils'. The devils are three masonry pillars and the pilgrims throw small pebbles at them as a symbolic gesture to cast out the 'devil within'.

The hajj ends with a ritual bath, the cutting or trimming of hair and the distribution of sacrificial meat, or the monetary equivalent, to the poor. On the tenth day of Dhul-Hijjah, Muslims all over the world join the pilgrims in Mecca to celebrate the completion of the hajj.

IMPORTANT DAYS IN THE MUSLIM CALENDAR

The *hijra*, the migration of the Prophet from Mecca to Medina, which falls on the eve of the first day of Muharram.
The Prophet's birthday, which falls on the eve of the twelfth day of Rabee' al-Awwal.
Eidul-Fitr, the celebration at the end of Ramadan, which falls on the first day of Shawwal.
Eidul-Adha, the day of the Arafat, the main event of hajj, which falls on the tenth day of Dhul-Hijjah.

In addition to the 'four pillars', jihad is also seen as a major obligation of a Muslim.

Jihad

Jihad is normally translated in English as 'holy war'. This is a perverse reduction of a highly spiritual, intellectual and social concept. Worse: in certain Muslim circles it has been reduced to mean war by any method, including terrorism. Nothing could be more distant from the essential meaning of jihad.

The word 'jihad' means 'to strive', 'to try one's utmost'. The Prophet Muhammad was asked: 'Who is the most excellent of all?' He replied: 'The believer who strives in the way of Allah with his person and his property.' Indeed, according to the Prophet there are four types of struggle that Muslims should engage in. The highest and the best jihad is jihad with one's self, the struggle with one's own ego. Then comes the struggle with one's wealth and intellect. These jihads are continuous processes. The struggle with one's greed, bad intentions and

lust is constant. Fighting economic injustice through philan-
thropic works is a never-ending exercise. Similarly, intellectual
jihad, standing up for truth and justice, is an endless requirement in a largely unjust world. 'A party of my community,' the
Prophet once declared, 'shall never cease struggling for the
truth.'

The fourth and final type of jihad is armed struggle. Jihad
can never take the form of aggression; indeed, the Qur'an
explicitly forbids aggression. It is undertaken against oppression
when all else fails. Strict rules have to be followed before jihad
can be declared. For example, jihad cannot be declared by one
group of Muslims against another. Neither can jihad be declared
unilaterally by one particular group. It has to be based on the
consensus of the entire community which must arise after wide
debate and discussion.

Moreover, jihad cannot be fought by any or all means. It
must be strictly fought according to the Islamic rules of engagement. These forbid killing women, children, old people and
non-combatants. Houses, cattle, trees, wildlife and the environment cannot be destroyed. And as far as kidnapping and acts
of terrorism that kill innocent people are concerned – they violate and do violence to every tenet of Islam.

That armed struggle plays a very minor role in jihad is well
illustrated by one of the sayings of the Prophet Muhammad.
The Prophet once asked a gathering: 'Whom would you count
to be a martyr among you?' The gathering replied: 'O
Messenger of Allah, whoever is killed fighting in the way of
Allah is a martyr.' 'In that case,' the Prophet replied, 'the
martyrs of my community shall be very few. He who dies in the
way of Allah is a martyr. He who dies a natural death in the way
of Allah is a martyr. He who dies of the plague in the way of
Allah is a martyr. He who dies of cholera in the way of Allah is

a martyr.' In other words, the way to paradise is to live a selfless, spiritual life devoted to good deeds.

Halal and Haram

What constitute good deeds? The Prophet Muhammad said, 'The world and all things in it are valuable.' Good works consist of maintaining the 'value' of the world. But, of course, the world does not stand still. So good works incorporate the idea of moving forward without damaging the world spiritually, physically, socially, culturally and politically. The Islamic term for justice, *adl*, includes the notion of displacement: a person or a thing that is displaced (or marginalized) is not in a state of adl. Adl requires for people and things, all that is in the world, to be accorded their proper value, to be in a state of harmony and grace. This is where the notions of *halal* and *haram* come in.

Literally, halal means permitted or praiseworthy, while haram has the meaning of forbidden or blameworthy. The term 'halal' has come to be associated with halal meat, the way animals are slaughtered for consumption in Muslim communities. But the concept is much broader and has a much greater significance. It implies behaving in a way that enhances the value of what one is doing, acting with due respect to oneself and others, giving proper due to community and society. In other words, promoting adl by doing good works. In Islam, all ways of knowing, being and doing that enhance the value of life and the material world, that promote justice and equality, are treated as halal. Outside this ethical framework where there is the danger of self-abuse, threat to life and environment and the spread of injustice, inequality and oppression is the haram, or forbidden, territory.

Like most religions, Islam forbids murder, rape, adultery,

incest and theft. But unlike most religions, usury (which includes earning interest) and alcohol (there is more harm in it than good, says the Qur'an) are also considered haram. Certain things which are haram become halal under particular circumstances: so you are allowed to eat carrion, which is strictly forbidden, if you are starving to death; and alcohol is permissible if you are dying of thirst and nothing else is available. However, the list of forbidden things is very short; and what is not forbidden is normally permitted.

But there is a problem. Apart from the general injunction to engage in good works, what is halal is left for Muslims, as individuals and communities, to discover for themselves. Thus, the constant challenge for Muslim people is to map out the halal territory most suitable for their era, to discover what actually enhances the value of life and the world. Is human cloning halal or haram? Can we consider globalization to be halal and therefore a praiseworthy trend? When does a thing that is halal actually become destructive and therefore has to be considered haram? Muslims, who have to make these decisions by consensus, have to constantly struggle with such questions.

Is the Veil Necessary?

One particular question that has become contentious in contemporary Islam is the issue of the veil. Many Muslims believe that it is absolutely essential for women to veil themselves. Indeed, for certain Muslim groups, particularly the traditionalists and puritans, it is a cardinal belief. But the veil, as modern Muslim women scholars have shown, is a pre-Islamic, upper-class custom that was later adopted in Muslim societies. The issue of the veil hinges around the famous modesty verses of the

Qur'an: 'Tell believing men to lower their gaze and be modest: that is purer for them. And tell believing women that they should lower their gaze and be modest, and to display of their adornment only that which is apparent, and to draw their veil over their bosoms . . .' (24:30–31) The verse unequivocally asks both men and women to observe modesty. But it has been given a patriarchal spin that puts the entire burden on women. Worse: 'modesty' has been interpreted to mean that women should cover themselves from head to toe and be completely shrouded.

During the time of the Prophet Muhammad, women moved freely in society. They prayed with men in the mosque, led prayers and played a leading part in public life. It was Caliph Umar who instituted segregated prayers, banned female imams and insisted that women should cover themselves. His successor, Othman, revoked many of these injunctions. But the veil has survived as an integral component of traditional, orthodox Islam. I see it as a perversion of the essentially egalitarian nature of Islam.

These, then, are some of the things that Muslims do and think about. But beyond the observances of 'the pillars of Islam', struggling with the notion of jihad and delineating what is halal and haram, there is a greater challenge. Muslims are urged to seek peace and justice by applying the principles of Islam to their own community and to society in general.

7

How Do You Apply Islam?

Islam is a highly social and political faith. Muslims, as I have constantly tried to argue, are required to pursue thought and learning and promote justice, equality and peace at every opportunity. To be a Muslim is to stand up for the oppressed and the marginalized. To practise Islam is to advance science and philosophy. But how you seek to apply Islam in your daily lives and your society depends very much on who you are.

For many Muslims, applying Islam simply means institutionalizing the Shariah. Indeed, since the 1950s when many Muslim countries acquired their independence, the Shariah has been at the top of the political agenda. But where the Shariah has been established as state law, it has led not to justice and equality but rather oppression and inequality. In countries like Saudi Arabia and Pakistan, the Shariah has been used to justify despotism, suppression of the freedom of expression, and criminal abuse of power.

This is largely because the Shariah has been drained of all its ethical and moral content. It has been reduced not just to 'law' but to a small number of legal precepts. These concern crime and punishment and regulation of social behaviour – the very aspects of the Shariah that are rooted in medieval interpretations. So establishing the Shariah simply means imposing laws concerning capital punishment, isolating women and banning all forms of entertainment.

Some Muslims think that the only way to apply Islam in the modern world is to establish an 'Islamic state'. This is a specific goal of those who follow various Islamic movements such as the Muslim Brotherhood of Egypt and Jamaat-e-Islami of Pakistan. These Muslims see 'Islam' and 'State' as a single entity, bound together by state law, the Shariah, and dominated by religious scholars. However, when religion, state and law become one and the same thing, Islam ceases to be Islam. It is transformed from a God-centred faith, a way of life and thought rooted in knowledge and action, to a totalitarian order that submits every human situation to the arbitration of the state. When Islam is transformed into an exclusivist ideology, the sacred is politicized and politics becomes sacred, everything is bulldozed into a quasi-fascist uniformity. This is why all modern 'Islamic states', such as Iran and Sudan, are totalitarian and monolithic in nature.

During the formative phase of Islamic history, Muslim communities were not too concerned with the Shariah. That concern appeared much later – around the fifteenth century. And it has become an obsession in much more recent times. But classical Muslim civilization sought to apply Islam through its key concepts.

What Are the Key Concepts of Islam?

The guidance provided by the Qur'an and the Sunnah, and even the Shariah, is rooted in certain ideas and values. These frame the worldview of Islam and constitute the building blocks of the culture and civilization.

The fundamental idea of the Islamic worldview is tawheed. Tawheed is normally translated as 'the Unity of God', but it also signifies the unity of humankind and the unity of people and nature. The world, according to Islam, is interconnected and exists in symbiosis.

Tawheed is intrinsically linked to the concept of khalifa. Khalifa means trustee, and men and women are described by Islam as trustees of God. Creation is a trust from God, and all of us, both as individuals and communities, are responsible for it, for looking after and caring for it until the time when the trust must be returned to its rightful owner.

The universe, then, according to Islam, is a unity emanating from a single will. And each individual human being is himself or herself a part of that world, dependent upon and related to all the other parts. Since both human beings and the universe are part of a single, continuing unity, the universe cannot be hostile to life or humanity. Neither can nature be held to be antagonistic towards humankind. Rather she is a friend whose purposes are at one with those of life and humanity. The task of human beings is not to contend with nature, not to seek to dominate her, for they have grown up in her bosom, and she and they together form a part of the single universe that proceeds from the single will. Thus, according to Islam, we live in a friendly environment which we must respect and care for.

The notions of tawheed and khalifa are combined with a string of other concepts and values to produce an integrated ethical framework. The responsibilities of the trusteeship, for example, are fulfilled on the basis of two other frequently mentioned concepts in the Qur'an: adl, or social justice, and *ilm* or knowledge. The thought of Muslims, that is the trustees of God, must be based on knowledge and the sole function of all their actions as trustees is to promote all-round justice. But the notions of adl and ilm are also subject to other ethical criteria. Justice and learning have to be sought on the basis of ijma (communal consensus), *shura* (consultation) and istislah (public interest). And Muslims are never allowed to forget that God seeks accountability not just in the Hereafter – *akhira* – but also here and now.

Let us briefly see how these concepts were applied in Islamic history, how the emphasis placed on them propelled the Muslim civilization to its zenith.

How Islam Has Been Applied in History

Consider the example of the Umayyad Caliph, Umar bin Abdul Aziz (681–720). By the time Umar became Caliph, Islam had spread as far as North Africa and Iran. He saw himself as a trustee of the state he ruled and insisted on consulting his people. Throughout his short rule of three years, he based his policies on public interest. He led a very austere existence, emphasized moderation and worried constantly about issues of equality and social justice. Once his wife found him weeping. 'What is the matter?' she asked. He replied, 'I have been made the ruler over the Muslims and minorities. I was thinking of the poor who are suffering, the sick who are destitute, the naked who are distressed, the oppressed who are stricken, the strangers who are in prison, and the venerable elders, and those with large families and small means, and I felt that God would ask an account of them at my hands on the Day of Judgement, and I feared that I would have no defence. So I wept.'

The Abbasid period, which is commonly regarded as the Golden Age of Islam, provides us with numerous other examples of the genuine application of Islam. The celebrated Caliph

Harun al-Rashid (786–809) equated his religion not with the state but with knowledge. A learned man who was fond of science and art, poetry and culture, he held philosophers and scientists in high regard. His concern for public interest led him to build schools and colleges, hospitals and dispensaries, and a string of roads, bridges and canals. He established the *Khizamat al-Hikmah*, the 'Library of Wisdom'; and public libraries, free and open to all citizens, became a common feature of the great cities of the Abbasid Caliphate.

His son al-Mamun (813–33) was even more learned than his father. The true happiness of Muslims, he declared, consisted in education and culture, so he spent most of his energies promoting science and learning. He initiated a massive movement for the translation of Greek and other foreign works in philosophy, science and medicine into Arabic. He went on to establish the famous *Bait al-Hikmah*, the 'House of Wisdom', in Baghdad in 830. The academy had a staff of eminent scientists and translators as well as copyists and binders. Among its employees were the Nestorian Christian Hunayn bin Ishaq and the Sabaean, Thabit ibn Qurrah – both became famous as translators and eminent scholars. Al-Mamun held regular discussions on literary, scientific and philosophical topics in his court. Every Tuesday, scholars from all over the empire, whatever their creed or race, gathered there to debate among themselves and with the Caliph. Blind faith and authoritarian theology, the Caliph announced, were worse than treason.

The emphasis on implementing concepts, rather than a reductive form of the Shariah, reveals Islam as an open system in theory. Indeed, it is only as an open system that Islam can really be applied in the contemporary world. While the ethical framework of Islam is established, the content of what constitutes 'Islam' in modern times is not an a priori given. It has to be argued. The Qur'an presents Islam as an argument: it constantly raises questions – philosophical, social, theological – that need to be addressed.

One of the most renowned theologians of Islam was Abu Hamid al-Ghazzali (d. 1111). A professor at the Nizamiyyah Academy in Baghdad, he suffered a spiritual crisis early in his life. This led him to the conclusion that religion could neither be proved nor disproved. 'No one believes,' he declared, 'unless they have doubted.' Al-Ghazzali argued that philosophy per se could not lead to happiness. Happiness required Muslims to rethink their religion. Consequently, he wrote his monumental work, *The Revival of Religious Knowledge in Islam*, which presents Islam in what was then a modern framework. With its synthesis of intellectual pursuits and religious concerns, the book had a tremendous impact on Muslim civilization. Later, he launched a major attack on philosophy in *The Incoherence of the Philosophers*.

In classical Islam, theologians constantly argued with philosophers about the nature of Islam and the meaning of a good and just life. Thus, al-Ghazzali's attack on philosophy did not go unnoticed. It was answered by ibn Rushd (d. 1198), who is known in the West as Averroes. Born in Córdoba, ibn Rushd is considered to be one of the greatest philosophers of all time. *The Incoherence of the Incoherence*, a point-by-point refutation of al-Ghazzali's arguments, is a truly monumental defence of rationalism.

What does an Islamic society look like? This was a major issue of contention between philosophers and theologians. Al-Farabi (d. 950), the philosopher who introduced Plato and Aristotle to Islam, sought a synthesis of Islam and Greek philosophy. While truth, and hence knowledge of God, can be attained by reason alone, he argued, we also need the moral framework of tawheed to attain true happiness. His work, *The Perfect State*, presents a synthesis of Platonic ideals and Islamic theology.

Ibn Rushd's friend and contemporary, ibn Tufail (d. 1185), argued that only knowledge can be a true guide to establishing an Islamic society, and we should allow knowledge to take us wherever it takes us. Ibn Tufail, who served as a Vizier at the Almohad court in Granada, was a champion of evolution. He is the author of the philosophical novel, *The Life of Hayy*. Hayy is 'spontaneously generated' on a desert island, learns to survive through observation and inference, and arrives at tawheed through rational deduction. The novel was translated into Latin and provided the inspiration for Daniel Defoe's *Robinson Crusoe*.

Muslim philosophers brought the moral and ethical precepts of Islam to their studies. For example, ibn Sina (d. 1037), one of the truly great philosophers of the world, wrote on poisons, but regarded experimentation with such substances as unethical. 'My science allows me to make poisons,' he said, 'but my religion does not permit their use.' Like most philosophers and scholars of Islam, ibn Sina was a polymath. He wrote on psychology, geology, mathematics, astronomy and logic. His immense encyclopaedic work, the *Kitab al-Shifa* (*The Book of Healing*), deals with these and many other subjects. His colossal medical treatise, *Canons of Medicine*, was a standard text – both in the Muslim world as well as Europe – for over six hundred years.

The scientists of classical Islam were deeply motivated by the idea of public interest, the notions of trusteeship and social justice. While they pursued knowledge for the sake of knowledge, they were also concerned with its social function. This is why they were obsessed with classification. Most Muslim scholars, from theologians to scientists and historians, produced their own classification of knowledge. Those of al-Kindi (d. 870), al-Ghazzali and Fakhr al-Din al-Razi (1149–1209), tried to identify knowledge that was essential for the survival of the community (e.g. medicine and astronomy) from merely trivial pursuits (e.g. astrology).

This concern for public interest and social justice led Muslim scientists to concentrate initially on developing knowledge that could serve the community. This is why most of the early work was done on mathematics and astronomy. Both had a direct bearing on Muslim society. Astronomy was needed to observe the new moon, as a navigational tool for pilgrims going to Mecca and to determine the time of prayers. Mathematics was needed for implementing the laws of inheritance, for promoting commerce and as a tool for astronomy.

Indeed, algebra was developed by al-Khawarizmi (d. 840) as an aid for calculating inheritance. In his *Book of Summary Concerning Calculating by Transposition and Reduction,* he shows how to perform basic mathematical functions, solve quadratic equations and so on.

Similarly, developments in mathematics and astronomy were designed to help travellers to Mecca as well as understand the cosmos. The astronomer al-Battani (d. 929), developed a string of trigonometrical formulae such as sine and cosine rules. Abu al-Wafa (d. 998) and ibn Yunus (d. 1009) developed the fundamental formula of spherical trigonometry in use today. One of the most eminent astronomers and mathematicians was Nasir al-Din al-Tusi (d. 1274), who managed the famous observatory at Maragha in Azerbaijan. Al-Tusi developed a mathematical device called the 'Tusi couple', which was essential in developing the heliocentric theory of the solar system. Later, ibn al-Shatir (d. 1375) developed a planetary theory that shares many features with that of Copernicus (d. 1543), who certainly knew of al-Shatir's work.

Medicine received special attention for the same reason. Hospitals, regulated and supervised by the state, had elaborate training programmes not just for doctors but also for pharmacists. Abu al-Qasim al-Zahrawi (d. 1013) published an illustrated encyclopaedia which described, amongst other things, the basic set of surgical instruments that are in use even today. Perhaps the greatest clinical doctor of Muslim civilization was Abu Bakr Zakariyya al-Razi (d. 925). A noted freethinker, al-Razi made the first detailed observations of smallpox and measles. His extensive writings include a monumental medical encyclopaedia.

But the notion of ilm meant that pure research could not be ignored either. Indeed, Muslim scientists were the first to establish experimentation as the basis for scientific method. This can be clearly seen in the work of ibn al-Haytham (d. 1039) and al-Khazini (d. 1121). Born in Basra, al-Haytham moved to Cairo with the intention of damming the Nile. As the job was beyond the reach of the technology of the time, he turned his attention to physics. In the *Book of Optics*, he presents optics both as a theoretical and experimental science; and he describes many basic laws of optics such as those of reflection and refraction. Al-Khazini constructed a special device for measuring specific gravity which he called the 'Balance of Wisdom'. In the book describing the device, he discusses mechanics, hydrostatics and a theory of gravity, identified as a central force directed towards the centre of the Universe (i.e. the Earth), centuries before Newton (d. 1727) encountered his falling apple.

The notions of adl, istislah and ilm demanded a universal system of education. So it is not surprising that early Muslim communities were very keen to establish universities and colleges. The first university in the world, al-Azhar, opened its gates in Cairo in 970. It was soon followed by other universities in Fez, Baghdad and as far as Samarkand.

The system of education that spread throughout the Muslim world provided travellers with a recognized intellectual passport. The personal history of innumerable Muslim travellers includes moving from the domain of one ruler to another and finding employment as a qadi, a judge. The renowned historian and father of sociology, Ibn Khaldun (d. 1406), lived in turbulent times that forced him to move between his native Tunisia, Morocco and Spain. He readily found employment as a qadi wherever he went. He is renowned for his multi-volume history of civilizations. The opening book, *Introduction to History*, is regarded as a masterpiece.

Travel was seen as essential for acquiring knowledge and seeing tawheed, the unity of humanity and nature, in action. It was also a direct response to the Prophet Muhammad's saying, 'Seek knowledge even (as far as) China.' The famous Muslim polymath, al-Baruni (d. 1048), did not go to China but India. Born in Khwarizm in Russia, al-Baruni was an astronomer, mathematician, geographer, historian, and social scientist. Every discipline, he declared, has its own methodology; and a scholar has to be true to the methodology of each discipline. He was among the first to devise methods for *The Determination of the Coordinates of the Cities*. But he is most famous for his enlightened study of India where he declares that to understand yoga you need to experience its method.

Ibn Battuta (d. 1377), on the other hand, did go to China. One of the greatest travellers of Islam, he served as a qadi in numerous places. He started his travels in 1325, and travelled for twenty-nine years the entire length and breadth of the known world, from China to Timbuktu. His rip-roaring adventures are describes in *Travels of Ibn Battuta*. Over four centuries earlier, ibn Fadhlan was sent as an emissary to Scandinavia by the Abbasid Caliph al-Muqtadir. He left Baghdad on 21 June 921, and returned with invaluable insights into the Vikings, and a swashbuckling story. His travels have been translated as *Eaters of the Dead* by Michael Crichton, and turned into a film, *The Thirteenth Warrior*.

Travellers, scholars, philosophers, scientists, theologians and even caliphs wrote books. Paper manufacturing, established in Baghdad in 793, provided the medium for the development of a book trade that played an essential part in the development of Muslim civilization. Every major city had a thriving book trade – at the time of al-Mamum, Baghdad alone had over a hundred bookshops. The most famous bookseller of Muslim civilization is ibn al-Nadim (d. 995). His bookshop in Baghdad was renowned throughout the empire. In 987, he published the *Fihrist*, a catalogue, which sought to provide an annotated bibliography of all the books in his shop, running to many thousands of entries. Entries noted the number of pages in the text so that purchasers could be sure they were not sold an abridged version.

For early Muslims, the concept of trusteeship had a particular environmental relevance. So they developed the notion of carrying capacity and built towns for a calculated number of people. They introduced 'inviolate zones' (known as *heram*) outside towns where development was forbidden. Another kind of inviolate zone (*hema*) was reserved for wildlife and forests. They formulated charters for animal rights, and declared that invaluable resources such as pasture, woodland, wildlife, mineral deposits and water could not be privately owned.

The classical period was also an era of intense debate and discussion about the interpretations of Islam. Sufis argued with religious scholars, both groups argued with philosophers, and everyone used philosophy as an instrument for presenting their case. The battle between the rationalist, known as the Mutazilites – literally the separatists – and religious scholars was particularly intense. It continued over several centuries. The Mutazilites, who tended largely to be philosophers but also included scientists, poets and administrators, desired a respectable distance between religion and politics. They were against strict, legalistic faith based solely on the notion of a Divine Law (the Shariah) and worked to transform Islam into a more humanistic religion. They argued that with reason alone one could know how to act morally; and by corollary, there was no necessity to combine religion and statecraft. The school emerged in the ninth century during the time of al-Kindi, known as 'the First Philosopher of the Arabs', who is accredited as its founder. The Mutazilites boosted such philosophers of distinction as al-Farabi, the tenth-century author of *The Perfect State* (which argued for a republic ruled by philosophers), ibn Sina and ibn Rushd.

The Mutazilites were pitted against the Asharites, founded by the tenth-century theologian al-Ashari. The Asharites rejected the idea that human reason alone can discern morality and argued that it was beyond human capability to understand the unique nature and characteristics of God. The state, the Asharites argued, had an important part to play in shaping the morality of its citizens; hence religion and politics could not be separated. The Asharites School had the support of giants like al-Ghazzali, Fakhr al-Din al-Razi and ibn Khaldun.

To a very large extent, the history of Islam during the classical period, from the seventh to the fourteenth centuries, can be seen as one gigantic struggle between the Mutazilites and the Asharites. It was the clear-cut victory of the Asharites that ensured that Muslim societies tended to see religion and politics as two sides of the same coin. The battle often went beyond the intellectual realm – if a particular caliph leaned on one side, he sometimes used his power to suppress the other side.

This is how Islam was applied in history. But all that was before decline and colonialism took their toll.

What Happened to Muslims in History

The conventional view is that Muslim civilization began to decline around the fifteenth century when the Ottomans were the dominant power in the Muslim world. The Ottomans, it is alleged, were too conscious of their military power and not interested in making contact with Europe or learning from its scientific advances. Consequently, science and learning went rapidly downhill.

The Ottoman Empire began in 1281. By the time of Sultan Suleiman I (1403–21), it stretched from the far shores of the Black Sea and the Persian Gulf in the east to Budapest in the north and Algiers in the west. They inherited, and were inspired by, the developments in science and learning that had taken place in Muslim civilization at its zenith. So they looked towards this rich tradition for solutions to their intellectual and technical problems. And, because they considered their own research and education systems to be self-sufficient, they were initially not keen on transferring science from Europe. Given that science in Europe and Islam were almost on a par at this stage in history, it made sense.

The sixteenth century was the golden age of the empire. The Ottoman chief astronomer, Taqi al-Din, illustrates this rather well. During the period of Sultan Murad III (1574–95), he built an observatory in Istanbul; it consisted of an elaborate structure and included, besides the observatory itself, residential quarters, offices for the astronomers, and a library. It was planned as one of the largest observatories in the Islamic world and was equipped with the best instruments of the time. Taqi al-Din's Istanbul observatory was comparable to Tycho Brahe's Uranienborg observatory built in 1576. Indeed, there are striking similarities between the instruments used by Tycho Brahe and those of Taqi al-Din. A particular kind of sextant built by Taqi al-Din resembled an instrument of the same type invented by Tycho Brahe.

During their peak, the Ottomans maintained an attitude of tolerance towards religious and ethnic minorities within their empire. The Jews, for example, were welcomed with open arms when they were banished from Spain at the end of the fifteenth century. But the Ottomans represented a particular threat to Europe: they were only just repelled from Vienna in 1683. Consequently, the Ottomans were portrayed as the darker side of Europe, the Other, and all the problems of Muslim societies were projected onto them.

The representation of the Ottomans – the Saracens as they were called in Europe – as violent, licentious fanatics was a new phase in an old cycle. Europe's ideas about Muslims and Islam have been fashioned and filtered through millennia of opposition, trepidation, false characterization and will to power – what has come to be known as Orientalism. Right from its inception, Islam presented Europe with three problems. First, what need was there for an Arabian prophet over six hundred years after the crucifixion and resurrection of God's own son? Second, when after one hundred years of its inception, Europe found Islam on its borders, it became a political problem. Third, the scientific and scholarly achievements of Muslim civilization made Islam an intellectual problem as well. All these problems were tackled by demonizing Islam, denigrating the Prophet Muhammad, and describing and representing Muslims as the opposite of Europe. So, if Europe was rational, Islam was irrational, if Europe was non-violent, Islam was violent, and if Europe was learned Muslims were ignorant.

Orientalism led Europe, which is so conscious of its own diversity, to consider Muslims and Islam as a monolith, a mass with no means for differentiation, diversity or dynamic interpretation. These representations reached their height during the Crusades; and they are still with us today. Indeed, it is the Orientalist stereotypes that are largely responsible for the widespread distrust of Muslims and misunderstanding of Islam.

They were used as partial justification for colonizing the Islamic world. Most of the Muslim world, with the exception of Turkey, was colonized by the European imperial powers. And wherever the Europeans went, they systematically dismantled the institutions of learning, suppressed original Islamic thinking and marginalized all those who could present an intellectual or political threat. In Algeria and Tunisia, for example, the French declared Islamic medicine to be inferior, introduced the death penalty for its practice and outlawed all Islamic doctors, the *hakims*. In Indonesia, the Dutch banned the local population from entering institutions of higher learning and denied education to most of the population till the 1950s. In India, the British set about creating a new breed of Indians who were 'English' in everything but their skin colour; and pitted the Hindus against the Muslims. Everywhere, the assets of the colonies were stripped, their economies were decimated, the social and cultural structures disbanded, and an inferiority complex engendered in the colonial subjects.

In an age when colonialism is being glorified on television, it is easy to underestimate its consequences. But more than anything else, it was colonialism that brought Islam to its knees. It was the prime external factor for the rapid decline of Muslim civilization.

Of course, internal factors also played their part. Prime among these were the intransigence of religious scholars, the *ulama*. Around the fourteenth century, the ulama became concerned at the proliferation of new, and often wild, interpretations of Islam. They worked ceaselessly, over a couple of centuries, to close the 'gates of *ijtihad*': it was not necessary, they argued, for Muslims to engage in continuous, 'sustained reasoning'. The way forward was taqlid or imitation of the thought and work of earlier generations of scholars. Ostensibly, this was a religious move. Taqlid was supposed to be limited to religious rulings. But given the fact that Islam is a highly integrated worldview, that in Islam everything is connected to everything else, it had a devastating impact on all forms of inquiry. Thus the dynamic principle of Islam, ijtihad, the notion that enables Islam to renew and revive it constantly, was outlawed. Later, fearing that they would lose control and their legitimacy over the exegesis of the Qur'an, the ulama also delayed the introduction of printing in Muslim societies.

The freezing of interpretation had a catastrophic effect on the development of Islamic thought. In particular, it stopped the evolution of the Shariah, which up to the fourteenth century was a dynamic, changing entity, in its tracks. The agency that individual Muslims had of interpreting and wrestling with their sacred text evaporated. On the whole, Muslims became empty vessels; all that was required of them was to accept classical rulings and devote themselves to the pursuit of rituals.

The intellectual, social, cultural and political devastation we see in the Muslim world today is essentially a product of the taqlidi mentality and the devastation wrought by colonialism.

How Islam Is Being Applied Today

Contemporary Muslim thinkers are beginning to see Islam in conceptual terms. Where possible, they use historic examples to shape contemporary ideas and policies. For example, the classical ideas on environmental husbandry are now widely employed in the Gulf States. Islamic Development Bank's 'Water for Living' project uses the notion of inviolate zones to promote conservation. The Birmingham-based Islamic Foundation for Ecology and Environmental Sciences has used Islamic concepts to introduce environmental ideas in the school curriculum.

Where history is silent, Muslim thinkers have created new discourses and disciplines. The contemporary notion of 'Islamic economics', for example, did not arise from within the classical tradition. While classical scholars discussed economic institutions, they did not develop an Islamic science of economics. Modern scholars, however, have used fundamental Islamic concepts to shape a modern discipline.

The central concept in Islamic economics is *falah*. Technically falah means a state of bliss. But it is a broad concept that refers to a comprehensive state of spiritual, cultural, political, social and economic well-being in this world and God's pleasure in the Hereafter. At a micro level, falah requires an individual to be gainfully employed, free from want, and to participate freely in social and political life. At a macro level, a society can attain falah if it is politically and economically independent, has institutional arrangements to establish economic justice, involves its people in decision-making and provides an environment congenial to physical and spiritual health.

The notion of falah has been used in conjunction with numerous other Islamic concepts to shape economic policies to eradicate poverty, meet basic needs and promote universal education.

As Islam forbids the earning of interest, models of interest-free banking have evolved. In the 1970s, Muslim countries launched a huge project to establish banking companies which would neither pay interest nor earn interest. Experiments soon led to two main forms of Islamic finance. Mudarabah involves banks going into partnership with businessmen and depositor and sharing profit. Murabaha involves the bank buying something on the specific request of a client and selling it to that client at a price higher than the purchase price, to be paid after a period of time. (Not surprisingly, some simply see this as interest with another name!) Islamic banks that operate on the principles of mudarabah and murabaha are now widespread throughout the Muslim world.

Similar conceptual analysis has been used to elucidate the idea of Islamic development. Here, the notion of trusteeship (khalifa) and falah are combined with a third concept: *tazkiyyah*. Tazkiyyah refers to the growth and purification of individuals in terms of their relationships with God, with their fellow humans and with the natural environment. Thus in Islamic development, growth is sought through purification, which paradoxically may involve giving away one's wealth. Moreover, wealth cannot be sought at the expense of the environment or accumulated to a level where it deprives others or undermines society as a whole. In other words, development has to operate within the principles of social justice. Moreover, development activities must take place within the boundaries of both a self-imposed and a socially enforced normative order.

The notion of Islamic development has also been formulated in a number of general policies. Some of those commonly referred to in the literature are:

1 production and consumption would be restricted to those goods and services which are deemed as useful for individuals and society;

2 efforts to improve the quality of life including employment creation, the institutionalization of zakat (poor tax), the equitable distribution of income and wealth through tax policies, inheritance laws, and the prohibition of usury, speculation and monopoly;

3 development should be along the lines of regional and sectoral equality to achieve a balanced development for the Muslim world;

4 technology must be suited to the conditions of specific Muslim societies and must, therefore, be in harmony with the goals and aspirations of the community without, at the same time, causing serious social disruption;

5 economic dependency on the non-Muslim world must be reduced and integration within the Muslim world must be brought about.

Both Islamic economics and Islamic development exist as independent disciplines with a vast body of literature. However, while models of Islamic economics have been generally accepted and widely promoted by Muslim countries, Islamic development does not command much support. Globalization, policies of international institutions such as the World Bank and the IMF, force Muslim countries to follow well-established patterns of western economic development.

The evolution of Islamic economics did, however, encourage Muslim thinkers to apply Islamic concepts to science policy. Indeed, an entire discourse of 'Islamic science' developed in the 1980s. In particular, this discourse combined the notion of knowledge (ilm) with the concept of ibadah or worship.

Scientific activity was projected as a form of worship. As worship, science also becomes a tool for the awareness of God (tawheed) and for the responsible exercise of being His trustee (khalifa). It follows that in an Islamic framework, science could not be involved in any acts of violence towards nature or, indeed, could it lead to waste, any form of oppression or tyranny (zulm) or be pursued for unworthy goals (haram). Both the ends and means of science had to be ethical. And it could only be based on praiseworthy goals (halal) on behalf of the public good (istislah) and the overall promotion of social, economic and cultural justice (adl).

Such a framework has strong implications for recent developments in genetic engineering, the patenting of biological material and vivisection. As a number of scholars have pointed out, Islamic science would be strongly in favour of the 'Precautionary Principle' and would only permit advances in genetic research on clearly delineated ethical principles. As it does not consider itself to be the only viable system of scientific advancement, it would respect and promote all forms of indigenous and alternative knowledge systems. In particular, it would encourage alternative and holistic systems of health.

One of the main purposes of the Islamic science debate is to internalize science within Muslim societies. The emphasis on indigenous research, it has been argued, should be on local problems that require urgent attention. So emphasis should be given to research into the prevention of diarrhoea rather than nuclear physics, or sanitation research instead of molecular biology. Given that almost three-quarters of all the political refugees in the world are Muslims, their problems should receive special attention. So developing materials for quick and clean temporary housing, efficient, cheap methods for supplying emergency water, mechanisms for providing basic health care and preventing the spread of diseases, and other systems for reducing the hardship and relieving the misery of the helpless and innocent victims of political turmoil, should be a high priority for science policies of Muslim states. Only by touching and transforming the lives of ordinary Muslims can science, advocates of Islamic science suggest, develop as a thriving enterprise in Muslim cultures.

There is one Islamic concept that is always in action in all Muslim societies. It is the notion of the ummah – the international brotherhood and sisterhood of Islam. The term ummah cannot be translated as 'people' or 'nation'. It is a much more organic and all-encompassing concept. It is best understood in the words of the Prophet Muhammad. 'The Muslims,' the Prophet said, 'are like a human body. If one part is in pain, the whole body suffers.' Muslims everywhere see themselves as an integral part of a larger whole. Every individual is a part of a community, and every community is part of a large international network of communities. So the problems of one community are the problems of the whole ummah.

This is why, for example, the issue of Palestine is not seen as an Arab or Middle Eastern problem, but a problem of the Muslim world itself. What happens in, or to, one Muslim community effects all Muslims, just as it would in an organic organism, the entire ummah. It has repercussions for the entire Muslim world. This is perhaps the best example of how Islamic consciousness manifests itself in the contemporary world.

Where Do Muslim Terrorists Come from?

There is another obvious way that Islam is being used today. The Islam of the terrorists – the 7/7 suicide bombers of

London, the hijackers of 9/11, and the al-Quaida/bin Laden network – is a particular sort of Islam. Most Muslims do not regard the terrorists as genuine Muslims, arguing that the Qur'an and various schools of Islamic law forbid the killing of innocent civilians. However, the terrorists are Muslims not simply because that's how they describe themselves but also because they justify their barbaric acts by reference to the same Qur'an and Islamic Law. Indeed, they are a product of Islamic history and a particular strand of its tradition. And they, too, are part of the ummah.

We came across this history in our discussion of the Kharjites, who first emerged during the period of the rightly guided caliphs. The Kharjites believed that the Qur'an should be interpreted literally, that no compromise, deviation or alternative can be permitted to this literal interpretation, and that all those who disagreed with them were legitimate targets for violence. The terrorists are the modern counterparts of the Kharjites. Like their predecessors, they have their own radical interpretation of Islam that is totally at odds with the dominant orthodoxy. Like their predecessors, the neo-Kharjites have no doubt that their identity is shaped by the best religion with the finest arrangements and precepts for all aspects of human existence; and there can be no deviation from the path. Those who do not agree are at best lesser Muslims and at worse legitimate targets for violence. In their rhetoric, all is sacred, nothing secular and retribution the paramount duty. Like the Kharjites, the modern-day Muslim terrorists justify their actions by invoking God's words and commands.

Although the Kharjites were eventually suppressed, their thought has recurred in Islamic history with cyclic regularity. They led several rebellions during the Abbasid period (749–1258) – the Golden Age of Islam. The influence of their thought can clearly be seen on Ibn Taymiyyah (1263–1328), the great-grandfather of Wahhabism, and one of the most influential political scientists of Islamic history. Kharjite thought is also evident in the ideas of Muhammad ibn Abdul Wahhab (1703–87), the founder of the Wahhabi sect, based in Saudi Arabia. It shaped the outlook of Syed Qutb (1906–66), the chief ideologue of the Muslim Brotherhood. His last work, *Milestones*, can be seen as a modern treatise on neo-Kharjite thought. Today, we can see their clear influence not just on those who subscribe to the bin Ladin doctrine, groups such as Hizb-e-Tahrir and al-Muhajaroon, but also on certain mainstream organizations, like the Jamaat-e-Islami of Pakistan.

Neo-Kharjite thought has three distinguishing features. First, it is ahistoric. It abhors history; and drains it of all humanity and human content. Islam as a religion, interpreted in the lives and thought of people called Muslims, is not something that unfolded in history with all its human strengths and weaknesses, but a utopia that exists outside time. Hence it has no notion of progress, moral development or human evolution. Its basic goal is the creation of an 'Islamic state', modelled on the historic utopia that is supposed to have existed during the time of the Prophet and the rightly guided caliphs, where religion and politics are one and the same thing.

Second, neo-Kharjite thought is monolithic. It does not recognize, understand or appreciate a contrary view. Those who express an alternative opinion are seen as apostates, collaborators or worse. The atrocities committed by Sunni extremists against the Shias in Iraq and Pakistan are justified in exactly these terms.

Third, this thought is aggressively self-righteous, and insists on imposing its notion of righteousness on others. It legitimizes intolerance and violence by endlessly quoting the famous verse from the Qur'an which asks the believers 'to do good and prevent evil deeds'. The Bali bombers of 2002 justified their actions with this verse. The Indonesian Front for the Defenders of Islam frequently burns and destroys cafés, cinemas and discos – places they consider to be sites of immoral or immodest behaviour. The hated religious police in Saudi Arabia are on the streets every day imposing a 'moral code' (mainly on women). In Pakistan, neo-Kharjite religious scholars succeeded in banning mixed – male and female – marathons.

What this means is that the neo-Kharjites have expunged Islam of all its humanity, history and ethics. On the whole, they have no conscience and feel no notion of guilt or remorse. They glorify their violence with the notions of martyrdom and speedy entrance to some perverted paradise.

8

Where Now?

Despite the emergence of a number of new ways of applying Islam, Muslims have, on the whole, failed to live up to the ideals and aspirations of Islam. Islam emphasizes thought and education. Yet, there is hardly a single reputable institution of higher learning in the Muslim world. Islam gives paramount importance to social justice, yet the Muslim world is awash with tyranny, despotism and oppression. Islam insists on the distribution of wealth and sees poverty as a sin, yet human degradation is a common sight in Muslim societies. Conspicuous wealth and abject poverty often exist side by side.

Muslims are prone to blaming the West for most of their problems. True, centuries of colonialism have left a deep scar on Muslim societies. And modern global economics together with Western hegemonic tendencies have also played a role in the underdevelopment of Muslim societies. But not all Muslim problems can be attributed to the West.

Failure to come to terms with modernity, I would suggest, is an important factor in the plight of contemporary Muslims. A tendency to fall back on age-old interpretations of sacred texts has kept them locked in the Middle Ages. Historic interpretations

constantly drag Muslims back to history, to the frozen and ossi-
fied context of long ago. Worse, the fundamentalists want to
take Islam back to the time of the Prophet Muhammad and the
rightly guided caliphs, a time imagined as a utopian nation
state but one that never even existed in history.

Muslims must now grasp the nettle and reformulate the
Shariah. As the central core of Islam, no reform is possible
without changing the Shariah. The evidence that Islam is now
undergoing serious reform comes from the fact that the very
idea that the Shariah is immutable and cannot be changed is
now being widely challenged. The Shariah, Muslim intellectuals and thinkers in places like Indonesia, Morocco and India are
arguing, is not divine. It is socially constructed in history. This
argument is a seismic shift. It will lead to a total transformation
of our understanding of Islam.

Indeed, this transformation has already begun. In Morocco,
for example, the Shariah has been totally reformulated. The
new Islamic Family Law, introduced in February 2004, sweeps
away centuries-old Islamic jurisprudence. Formulated with the
full cooperation of religious scholars and the active participation
of women, it introduces many profound changes. But every
change is justified – chapter and verse – from the Qur'an, and
from the examples and traditions of the Prophet Muhammad.

So, what are these changes?

The traditional Shariah notion that the husband is the head
of the family has gone, to be replaced by the notion of the
family as the joint responsibility of both spouses. The debasing
language previously used in reference to women has been
replaced with gender-sensitive terminology. So, women become
men's partners in rights and obligation rather than their under-
lings in need of guidance and protection. The marriageable
age for women has been raised from fifteen to eighteen,

bringing it up to par with men's. Women and men now have the right to contract their own marriage without the legal approval of a guardian. Women have the right to divorce; and the conventional Shariah notion that men have a unilateral right to divorce has been ditched. Men now require prior authorization from a court before they can obtain a divorce. Verbal divorce has also been outlawed.

Moreover, husbands are required to pay all monies owed to the wife and children in full, before a divorce can be duly registered. Polygamy has been all but abolished. Men can take second wives only with the full consent of the first wife and only if they can prove, in a court of law, that they can treat them both with absolute justice – an impossible condition. Women can now claim alimony and can be granted custody of their children even if they remarry. Indeed, a woman can even regain custody of her children if the courts initially ruled in favour of the husband but the husband failed to fulfil his responsibilities.

There is also provision for the child to get suitable accommodation consistent with his or her living conditions prior to the parents' divorce. This requirement is separate from the other alimony obligations, which conventionally consisted of a paltry lump sum. Also recognized is the child's right to acknowledgement of paternity where the marriage has not been officially registered or the child was born out of wedlock.

The new law also requires that husbands and wives share the property acquired during marriage. Husbands and wives can have separate estates but the law makes it possible for the couple to agree, in a document other than the marriage contract, on how to manage and develop assets acquired during marriage. The traditional tribal custom of favouring male heirs in the sharing of inherited land has also been dropped, making it possible for the grandchildren on the daughter's side to inherit from their grandfather, just like the grandchildren on the son's side.

Under the reformulated Shariah, minorities are allowed to follow their own laws. So Moroccan Jews are allowed to be governed by the provisions of the Hebraic Moroccan Family Law.

These are profound shifts. They demonstrate that the Shariah can be radically transformed. While these profound changes are limited to the family law aspect of the Shariah, they will have an impact on the Shariah as a whole. Reforms of other aspects of the Shariah, including crime and punishment, which is even more contentious, will no doubt follow.

An indication of this is provided in Malaysia and Indonesia. In Malaysia, a new interpretation of Islam, called 'Islam Hadhari', has emerged. Drawing its inspiration from ibn Khaldun, the fourteenth-century Muslim historian and founder of sociology, it is rooted in the civilizational and cultural aspects of Islam. The emphasis is on the central role of knowledge in Islam. Muslim societies, the proponents of Islam Hadhari argue, should be knowledge-based societies. They should value intellectual labour, economic development and scientific and technological innovation. And Muslims should be 'inclusive' – tolerant and outward-looking towards other faiths and ideologies.

In Indonesia, traditional and modern groups have joined together to produce a new synthesis. The 'new Islamic intellectualism', as it is called, aims to separate the Shariah from the political realm. The Shariah, it is argued, cannot be the law of the state. Its overemphasis on formality and symbolism has drained the Shariah, and hence Islam, of its ethical and humane dimension. Muslims should aim to rediscover the values and ethics of the Shariah and use it to promote civic society and participatory and accountable governance. And this should be done from the grass roots, with full participation of all members of society.

What's happening in Indonesia, Malaysia and Morocco is by no means unique. Similar developments are taking place right across the Muslim world. Muslims, generally, are acknowledging the need for fundamental change in their perception of Islam. Conscious efforts are being made to move away from the medieval notions of Islamic law and implement the vision of justice, equality and beauty that is rooted in the Qur'an. If these changes continue, the future will not repeat the recent past.

Islam in the Twenty-first Century

The new reformist agenda is setting up Islam for a vibrant future. 'Formalized Islam', as the Indonesian intellectuals describe it, will always be with us. But this vision of Islam, so rooted in legalism, so exclusivist, so myopic, will lose much of its appeal and force.

There are two basic drivers of change: women and youth. The reforms in Islamic law in Morocco were led largely by women. Over the last few decades, a whole generation of female scholars has emerged, who are now reinterpreting the Qur'an. Scholars like Fatima Mernissi, Asma Barlas, Amina Wadud and Aisha Abdul Rahman are transforming the theological landscape. The efforts for liberal and humanistic interpretations of Islam are led by young thinkers. For example, the Indonesian liberal Islam network, which is a mass movement, is led almost exclusively by writers and theologians in their thirties. In addition, there is one other instrument of change that cannot be overlooked: globalization. Whatever the pros and cons of globalization, its economic benefits in countries like Pakistan and India are producing a more articulate, modern and aware middle class with a deep dislike of conservative orthodoxy. This emerging class will not only demand but will actually usher in change.

On the other side of the equation, the fundamentalists will become superfluous. Fundamentalist discourse is all slogans and no programme. It sets a false agenda of peripheral issues and perpetual conflict. This is why there is such widespread repugnance against fundamentalism in the Muslim world. In the next decade or so, this aversion will become an unstoppable tide. But fundamentalism will not be overwhelmed by liberal or moderate Muslims. It will implode due to its own viciousness and vacuous nature.

The various efforts to reinterpret Islam are attempts to come to terms with two basic issues. How are Muslims to transcend their fossilized tradition and reinvent this tradition as a life-enhancing force? And how can Muslim civilization rediscover its dynamism and élan?

There are no ready-made answers to these questions. Indeed, the questions seem particularly formidable given the state of education in the Muslim world.

But the important thing to realize is that Muslims are now asking appropriate questions. The answers will lead us to the discovery of a new Islamic paradigm. Thus the basis for changing the reality of Muslims in the modern world will be recognized; and the foundation for creating a distinctively different future for Muslim civilization will be established.

So prepare yourself for the re-emergence of a dynamic, thriving civilization for Islam. It will not emerge in the near future. It will take several decades, even half a century. It will be deeply rooted in history and tradition, but it will be a totally different entity. It will demonstrate that liberal humanism is not a Western invention; rather it has deep roots in Islamic history. It will show that pluralism is not a gift of secularism. Rather pluralism and diversity are intrinsic to the worldview of Islam. It will not be 'modern' in the Western sense of the world. And it will not be for or against the West. Rather it will be across and above the West. And it will demonstrate that, even in a globalized world, diversity and difference matter, and can lead to fruitful synthesis.

Thus the future is not riddled with conflicts between Islam and the West, or with traditionalism and secularism. On the contrary, the future will be shaped by mutual respect and collaboration. And it will be a multi-civilizational future where the two civilizations – and others, such as China and India – will nourish themselves from their distinct ways of being.

Is my vision of the future too optimistic? Am I too eager to sweep away the contentious issues, the areas of possible conflict? How one sees the future depends on how one sees the present. And how one sees the present depends very much where one looks. We need to redirect our gaze away from the hateful fundamentalists and towards all those who are earnestly trying to reconstruct Muslim civilization. Despite serious hurdles, this project is on its way.

Besides, Islam does not permit one to be a pessimist. Religion in general, and Islam in particular, is all about hope. Hope in the mercy and beneficence of God. Hope in the goodness and pragmatic sense of humanity. Optimism is thus an essential part of Islam. To be a Muslim is to be a cautious but eternal optimist.

What is quite evident is that Muslims are thinking of the future as a space for contemplating the consequences of present action. In developing new interpretations of Islam, and attempting to reform the Shariah, they seek to develop an ethically disciplined vision of the future. It is only through the wise contemplation of the future that Muslims will realize their deepest aspirations – and return, once again, to the enlightened social vision and humane spirit of Islam.

This is what I, as a Muslim, believe. But only God knows best. In the end, as in the beginning, all praise is due to Him.

Glossary

Adl: justice, more particularly, distributive justice in all its various manifestations: social, economic, political, environmental as well as intellectual and spiritual.

Akhira: life after death, the Hereafter, when each person will be asked to account for his or her deeds. Refers to another existence after the life of the world, an existence which is shaped by a person's conduct in this life. The concept involves the notion of accountability: we are accountable before God for all our thoughts and actions. The Hereafter begins with the Day of Resurrection, which is followed by the Day of Judgement.

Allah: literally 'the God', Who has no gender and cannot be imagined by the human mind but can only be understood through His attributes.

Din: Islam's description of itself. In its primary sense *din* means a return to man's inherent nature. In general, *din* not only includes the idea of religion as commonly understood, but also the notions of culture, civilization, tradition and worldview.

Dhikr: remembrance of God. Very common in Sufi practice.

Fard: obligation, compulsory duty. Refers to individual as well as social and collective obligations such as daily prayers. *Fard ayn* is duty imposed on responsible individuals; *fard kifaayah* is the duty imposed on the Muslim community. Both kinds of obligation have to be met for a successful and happy life.

Fiqh: Islamic jurisprudence. The bulk of the Shariah, Islamic Law, is in fact *fiqh*, which consists largely of the opinion of classical jurists.

Fitra: the primordial nature of human beings. Islam describes itself as *din al-fitrah*, the natural way of life.

Haddud: literally limits or boundaries which cannot be exceeded. Normally refers to the crime and punishment part of the Shariah which are themselves called *haddud*. Under *haddud*, punishment is handed out according to fixed laws. This is the most contentious part of the Shariah.

Hadith: sayings or traditions of the Prophet Muhammad.

Halal: lawful, good and beneficial.

Hajj: pilgrimage to Mecca, one of the Pillars of Islam, performed during a particular moment of the Islamic year.

Haram: unlawful, and socially, morally and spiritually harmful.

Hijra: the migration of the Prophet Muhammad from Makkah to Medina in the twelfth year of his mission in July 622. It marks the beginning of the Islamic calendar (the years AH), which is thus referred to as the Hijra calendar.

Ibadah: worship. *Ibadah* is not limited to ritual worship but incorporates all activities undertaken to seek the pleasure of God. Thus the pursuit of knowledge, earning one's livelihood by just and moral means, helping other people, leading one's community with humility and by fair and just means – are all acts of *ibadah*.

Ijma: literally agreeing upon, consensus of the community in general, and the learned in particular. One of the four bases of Islamic Law.

Ijtihad: systematic original thinking; exerting oneself to the utmost degree to reach comprehension and form an opinion. *Ijtihad* gives Islam an intrinsic dynamism but its exercise requires fulfilment of certain stringent criteria. The 'gates of *ijtihad*' were closed by religious scholars in the Middle Ages.

Ilm: knowledge in all forms, and distributive knowledge in particular; it incorporates the notion of wisdom and justice.

Islam: peace, submission to God, religion of God, the natural inclination of human beings.

Istislah: public interest. A supplementary source of Islam law.

Jihad: literally striving. Any earnest striving in the way of God, involving personal, financial, intellectual or physical effort, for righteousness and against oppression or wrong doing.

Khalifa: trusteeship. The Qur'an describes a man or a woman as a *khalifa*, a steward or trustee of God on earth. Earth's resources are a trust from God and the trustees are responsible for how the trust is managed. The term *khalifa* (caliph) has also been used to describe the head of a Muslim state. In particular, the term was used after the death of the Prophet Muhammad to describe his successors.

Mudarabah: profit-sharing. A key term in Islamic economics, it has become the basis for 'interest-free banking'.

Salah: daily obligatory prayer. The prime content of these prayers is recitation of some verses of the Qur'an, or as it has been called the repetition of God's words within oneself in acknowledgement that only God can adequately praise Himself.

Seerah: the life or biography of the Prophet Muhammad.

Shariah: literally means the path to a watering hole; it is the ethical, moral and legal code of Islam. Conventionally translated as 'Islamic Law'.

Shura: cooperation and consultation for the benefit of the community; more particularly consultation as a political principle.

Sufi: a Muslim mystic.

Sunnah: literally path or example. Applies particularly to the example of the Prophet Muhammad and includes what he said, actually did and agreed to.

Taqlid: imitation, particularly on religious matters, of the rulings and opinions of classical religious scholars.

Tawheed: belief in the affirmation of Oneness of God.

Ulama: religious scholars, a dominant class in Muslim society.

Ummah: the ensemble of Muslim individuals and communities forming an entity of common culture with common goals and aspirations, as well as a certain self-consciousness, but not necessarily a unified common polity.

Zakat: the compulsory purifying tax on wealth.

A Selection from the Qur'an

There is no compulsion in religion.
(2:256)

Say: 'God is unique!' God, the Source (for everything). He has not
fathered anything nor is He fathered, and there is nothing comparable to Him.
(112:1–4)

Say: 'We believe in God and what was sent down to us and what was
sent down to Abraham, Ishmael, Isaac, Jacob, and the Tribes, and
what was given to Moses, Jesus and all the prophets by their Lord. We
make no distinction between any of them, and we devote ourselves to
Him.'
(2:136)

We have created you all out of a male and a female, and have made
you into nations and tribes, so that you might know one another.
(49:13)

We created man from an extract of clay; then We placed him as a drop
of semen in a safe resting place. Then We turned the semen into a
clot; next We turned the clot into tissue; and We turned the tissue
into bones and clothed with flesh. Then We performed creation all
over again. Blessed be God, the best Creator.
(23:12–14)

God commands justice, doing good, and generosity towards relatives and He forbids what is shameful, blameworthy and oppressive.
(16:90)

You who believe, be steadfast in your devotion to God and bear witness impartially: do not let hatred of others lead you away from justice, but adhere to justice, for that is closer to the awareness of God.
(5:8)

Do not mix truth with falsehood, nor knowingly conceal the truth.
(2:42)

Help one another to do what is right and good; do not help one another towards sin and hostility.
(5:2)

Be tolerant and command what is right: pay no attention to foolish people.
(7:199)

What about someone who worships devoutly during the night, bowing down, standing in prayer, ever mindful of the life to come, hoping for His Lord's mercy? Say: 'How can those who know be equal to those who do not know?' Only those who have understanding will take heed.
(39:9)

Say: 'Lord, increase me in knowledge.'
(20:127)

There are signs in the heavens and the earth for those who believe: in the creation of you, in the creation God scattered on earth, there are signs for people of sure faith; in the alternation of night and day, in the rain God provides, sending it down from the sky and reviving

the dead earth with it, and in the shifting of the winds there are signs for those who use reason.
(45:28)

The worst creatures in God's eye are those who are (wilfully) deaf and dumb, who do not use reason.
(8:22)

Travel throughout the earth and see how He brings life into being.
(29:20)

Be good to your parents, to relatives, to orphans, to the needy, to neighbours near and far, to travellers in need, and to your selves. God does not like arrogant, boastful people, who are miserly and order other people to be the same, hiding the bounty God has given them.
(4:36)

Seek help with steadfastness and prayer – though this is hard indeed for anyone but the humble, who know that they will meet their Lord and unto Him they will return.
(2:45)

A kind word and forgiveness is better than a charitable deed followed by hurtful words.
(2:263)

Give full measure: do not sell others short. Weigh with correct scales: do not deprive people of what is theirs. Do not spread corruption on earth.
(26:181–3)

God does not change the condition of a people until they change their own condition.
(13:11)

There is an appointed time for every people: they cannot hasten it, nor, when their time comes, will they be able to delay it for a single moment.
(7:34)

I swear by the glow of sunset, by the night and what it covers, by the full moon, you will progress from stage to stage.
(84:16–19)

The present world is only an illusory pleasure.
(3:185)

A Selection from the Hadith

God is pure and loves purity and cleanliness.

The world is green and beautiful and God has appointed you His stewards over it.

The whole earth has been created a place of worship, pure and clean.

Whosoever plants a tree and diligently looks after it until it matures and bears fruit is rewarded.

Every religion has a special character; and the characteristic of Islam is modesty.

The best richness is the richness of the soul, the best provision is piety, the most profound philosophy is the fear of God.

Do you love God? Love your fellow being first.

If a person loves his brother, he should tell him so.

No man is a true believer unless he desires for his brother what he desires for himself.

The servants of God are those who walk the earth in humility.

Kindness is a mark of faith; those without kindness are also without faith.

Gentleness adorns everything and its absence leaves everything tainted.

Have compassion on those who live on Earth and He Who is in Heaven will have compassion on you.

The most excellent jihad is the conquest of one's own ego.

Be not angry.

Strive always to excel in virtue and truth.

Say what is true, although it may be bitter and displeasing to people.

He is not one of us who does not show kindness to children and respect to elders.

Sit together and eat in company.

Give the labourer his wage before his perspiration dries.

Do not monopolize.

The truthful and trustworthy merchant is associated with prophets, martyrs and the upright.

The little but sufficient is better than the abundant and alluring.

Look towards those who are less fortunate than yourself; it is best for you, so that you may not hold God's benefit in contempt.

Charity is incumbent upon every human limb every day upon which the sun rises.

Doing justice is charity; and assisting a man upon his beast and lifting his baggage is charity; and pure, comforting words are charity; and answering a questioner with mildness is charity; and removing that which is an inconvenience to wayfarers, such as thorns and stones, is charity.

Feed the hungry and visit the sick, free the captive if he is unjustly confined, and assist the oppressed.

God has not created anything better than reason or anything more perfect and beautiful than reason.

Seek knowledge from the cradle to the grave.

An hour's contemplation is better than a year's worship.

He who knows his own self knows God.

Learn to know thyself.

The ink of the scholar is more holy than the blood of the martyr.

Who are the learned? Those who practise what they know.

Wealth comes not from the abundance of worldly goods, but from the contentment of the mind.

Safeguard yourself against miserliness, for it ruined those who were before you.

Beware of envy, for envy devours good works as fire devours fuel.

Beware of suspicion, for suspicion is a great falsehood.

Do not search for faults in each other nor yearn after that which others possess, nor envy and entertain malice or indifference.

God does not look upon your bodies and appearances, He looks upon your hearts and your deeds.

Make things easy and do not make them hard, and cheer people up and do not rebuff them.

Rejoice and hope for that which will please you.

Further Reading

The Qur'an: A New Translation, M. A. S. Abdel Haleem, Oxford University Press, 2004.

Discovering the Qur'an: A Contemporary Approach to a Veiled Text, Neal Robinson, SCM Press, London, 1996.

Qur'an, Liberation and Pluralism, Farid Esack, Oneworld, Oxford, 1997.

Muhammad: A Biography of the Prophet, Karen Armstrong, Weidenfeld & Nicholson, London, 2001.

The Prophet Muhammad: A Biography, Barnaby Rogerson, Little, Brown, London, 2003.

Introducing Islam, Ziauddin Sardar and Zafar Abbas Malik, Icon Books, Cambridge, 2002.

No God But God, Reza Aslan, William Heinemann, London, 2005.

Islamic Humanism, Lenn E. Goodman, Oxford University Press Inc., USA, 2003.

Qur'an and Women, Amina Wadud, Oxford University Press, USA, 1999.

Women and Islam, Fatima Mernissi, Blackwell, Oxford, 1991.

Women Claim Islam, Miriam Cooke, Routledge, London, 2000.

Orientalism, Ziauddin Sardar, Open University Press, Buckingham, 1999.

Desperately Seeking Paradise: Journeys of a Sceptical Muslim, Ziauddin Sardar, Granta Books, 2004.

A Fundamental Fear: Eurocentrism and the Emergence of Islamism, Bobby S. Sayyid, Zed Books, London, 1997.

Islamic Science and Engineering, Donald R. Hill, Edinburgh University Press, 1994.

The Venture of Islam, Marshall Hodgson, Chicago University Press, 1975 (3 vols.).

Muslim Networks from Hajj to Hip Hop, ed. by Miriam Cooke and Bruce B. Lawrence, University of North Carolina Press, Chapel Hill, 2005.

The Case for Islamo-Christian Civilization, Richard W. Bulliet, Colombia University Press, New York, 2004.

Contacts Listing

The Islamic Foundation
Markfield Conference Centre
Ratby Lane, Markfield
Leicester LE67 9SY
Tel: +44 1530 244 944
email: i.found@islamic-foundation.org.uk
www.islamic-foundation.org.uk

NORTH AMERICA
Islamic Society of North America
PO BOX 38
Plainfields, IN 46168, USA
Tel: +1 317 839 8157
email: info@isna.org
www.isna.net

The Council of American-Islamic Relations
453 New Jersey Avenue S.E., Washington, DC 20003–4034, USA
Tel: +1 202 488 8787
email: webmaster@cair-net.org
www.cair.net.org

Canadian Islamic Congress
675 Queen St S., Suite 208
Kitchener, Ontario N2M 1A1, Canada
Tel: +1 519 746 1242
email: cic@canadianislamiccongress.com
www.canadianislamiccongress.com

Canadian-Muslim Civil Liberties Association
885 Progress Ave., Suite UPH14, Toronto, Ontario M1H 3G3,
Canada
Tel: +1 416 289 3871
email: cmcla@cmcla.org
www.cmcla.org

Muslim Canadian Congress
12 Millington Street
Toronto, Ontario M4X 1W8, Canada
Tel: +1 416 928 0477
email: muslimchronicle@canada.com
www.muslimcanadiancongress.org

AUSTRALIA
The Australian Federation of Islamic Councils
P.O. Box 7185, South Sydney Business Hub
Alexandria, NSW 2017
Australia
Tel: +612 9319 6733
email: admin@afic.com.au
www.afic.com.au

IRELAND
The Islamic Foundation of Ireland
163 South Circular Road, Dublin 8
Tel: +353 453 3242
email: ifi@indigo.ie

Websites

There are numerous websites that provide information on Islam, with a huge number focused exclusively on debate and discussion of Islamic issues. The following are the ones that I have found useful:

www.islamonline.net
One of the biggest and most active, the Internet equivalent of al-Jazeera TV, it includes live question-and-answer sessions

www.islamicity.com
Good on resourceful, background material on Islam, and live TV

www.muslimheritage.com
Lively, well-illustrated site on the history of science and technology in
Islam

http://muslimwakeup.com/
Maintained by the Progressive Muslim Union of America, this site is
devoted largely to issues of internal reform within Islam

Index

BOCA RATON PUBLIC LIBRARY, FLORIDA

3 3656 0387028 9

297 Sar
Sardar, Ziauddin.
What do Muslims believe? :